Supercrit #4
Bernard Tschumi
Parc de la Villette

09

'Tschumi embraced the Supercrit experience with all the diligence of a final year student, arriving half an hour early and rearranging all the drawings for the jury's and audience's scrutiny ... Tschumi's presentation was a tour de force ...' Helen Castle, editor of Architectural Design

'The explicit instruction in the competition brief was that this scheme was not to be a post-modernised park ... La Villette was one of those flowers that sprang out of the ruins, or the demolition, of these old ideas.' Paul Finch (OBE)

'The great thing about the fact that [Tschumi] won the competition is that it showed the profession that somebody who can teach and draw and write, can build ...' Peter Cook, Archigram

'... I think it is a piece of artwork. It is quite inspirational ...' Bruce McLean, artist

The Supercrit series revisits some of the most influential architectural projects of the recent past and examines their impact on the way we think and design today. Based on live studio debates between protagonists and critics, the books describe, explore and criticise these major projects. Supported by an extensive illustrated section describing the project itself and a wider selection of pictures describing the wider context of the debate, these books are aimed at both a new and an expert audience. While introducing the projects themselves to newcomers, with original descriptions and adding generous footnotes and sources to a full transcript of the debate, they are also an important contribution to the ongoing discussion which surrounds these seminal projects.

Supercrit #4: Parc de la Villette examines the groundbreaking public space with art installations. You can hear the architect's project definition, see the drawings and join in the crit. This innovative and compelling book is an invaluable resource for any architecture student.

Samantha Hardingham is an architectural writer and researcher, and teaches at the Architectural Association. She was Senior Research Fellow in the Research Centre for Experimental Practice at the University of Westminster 2003-8. Her published works include several editions of London: A Guide to Recent Architecture (ellipsis, 1994–2002) which pioneered a new series of architecture guides, Cedric Price Opera (Academy Wiley, 2003), Experiments in Architecture (august projects, 2005) and Cedric Price Retriever (Iniva, 2006).

Kester Rattenbury is an architectural journalist, writer and teacher, and co-ordinates the Research Centre for Experimental Practice at the University of Westminster, where she is Reader in Architecture and was principal investigator on the Archigram Archival Project (2010). She has written, co-written and edited books including This is Not Architecture (Routledge, 2002), Architects Today (Lawrence King, 2004) and the Supercrit series.

Supercrit #4
Bernard Tschumi
Parc de la Villette

Samantha Hardingham and Kester Rattenbury

First published 2012
by Routledge
2 Park Square, Milton Park, Abingdon,
Oxon, OX14 4RN

Simultaneously published in the USA
and Canada by Routledge
711 Third Avenue, New York, NY 10017

Routledge is an imprint of the Taylor &
Francis Group, an informa business

British Library
Cataloguing in Publication Data
A catalogue record for this book is available
from the British Library

Library of Congress
Cataloging-in-Publication Data
Hardingham, Samantha.
Bernard Tschumi : Parc de la Villette /
Samantha Hardingham and Kester
Rattenbury.
    p. cm. — (Supercrit ; #4)
Includes bibliographical references and
index.
1. Parc de La Villette (Paris, France) 2.
Tschumi, Bernard, 1944-—Criticism and
interpretation. 3. Deconstructivism
(Architecture)—France—Paris. 4. Cultural
parks—France—Paris. 5. Parks (France)—
Buildings, structures, etc. I. Rattenbury,
Kester. II. Title. III. Title: Parc de la Villette.
    SB485.P24H37 2011
    720.92—dc22
                        2010019461

ISBN: 978-0-415-45787-3 (hbk)
ISBN: 978-0-415-45788-0 (pbk)

Original text design and cover design by
John Morgan Studio
Typesetting and layout by Alex Lazarou

Contents

SUPERCRIT DEFINITION

a. Supercrits take major experimental projects that have 'changed the weather' of architectural thought and practice – and put them back into the teaching studio 'crit' format for open public and expert debate.

b. Supercrits were devised by EXP, the Research Centre for Experimental Practice, Department of Architecture, University of Westminster, London. EXP assert their copyright of the name and idea.

c. Projects selected should have been innovative in their time and have continued to influence architectural culture, practice and thought. They may be built or unbuilt, temporary or permanent, and may include books, exhibitions and events as well as buildings or master plans.

d. Wherever possible, the original protagonists are invited to present their projects, considering them both in the context of the time and with hindsight.

e. Speakers present their project to a panel of international critics and to an open audience of students, professionals and an interested public. Selection of critics and guests aims to generate debate both in the context of the time and in terms of subsequent and contemporary influence.

f. Partners: Supercrits have been supported by a variety of organisations in a range of ways. From Supercrit #3, the series has been co-run with the Architecture Foundation.

g. Venue: usually (but not exclusively) the University of Westminster, 35 Marylebone Road, London.

h. Timing: usually (but not exclusively) 10.00–12.30, Wednesday or Friday mornings.

i. Access: Supercrits are free and open to the public. Seats must be reserved.

j. Events to date have been:
    Supercrit #1: Cedric Price, 'POTTERIES THINKBELT', 5 November 2003
    Supercrit #2: Robert Venturi and Denise Scott Brown, 'Learning from Learning from Las Vegas', 16 March 2004
    Supercrit #3: Richard Rogers, 'The Pompidou Centre', 22 April 2005
    Supercrit #4: Bernard Tschumi, 'Parc de la Villette', 14 October 2005
    Supercrit #5: Rem Koolhaas, 'Delirious New York', 5 May 2006
    Supercrit #6: Leon Krier, 'Poundbury', 31 October 2008

PROJECT DATA

Project name   Parc de la Villette

Site   125 acres or 55 hectares (approximately), 19th Arrondissement in the north west of Paris where the Quai de l'Oise meets the Boulevard Périphérique

International competition   1982–3

Client   The French Government, The Ministry of Culture, Serge Goldberg – President of the Etablissement Public du Parc de la Villette, François Barré – Directeur du Parc

Construction   1985–98

Architects   Bernard Tschumi Architects (BTA)

Invited protaganists of built and unbuilt garden, folie and furniture designs

BUILT: Alexandre Chemetoff, Daniel Buren & Bernhard Leitner; Giles Vexlard & Laurence Vacherot; Jean-Max Albert; Claes Oldenburg & Coosje van Bruggen; Philippe Stark; Fujiko Nakaya; Alain Pélissier

UNBUILT: Jean Nouvel; John Hejduk; Peter Eisenman & Jaques Derrida; Michel Butor & Henri Pousseur: Henri Gaudin; Gaetano Pesce; Cedric Price; Kathryn Gustafson; Jean Magerand & Elisabeth Mortamais; Paysages

Project staff   COMPETITION: Bernard Tschumi, Luca Merlini, Alexandra Villegas, Luca Pagnamenta, Jon Olsen

CONSULTANTS: Galen Cranz, Phoebe Cutler, William Wallis, Thomas Balsey

PROJECT: Bernard Tschumi, Jean-François Erhel, Ursula Kerz, Luca Merlini, Alexandra Villegas, Christian Biecher, Marie-Line Luquet, Neil Porter, Steve McAdam, Luca Pagnamenta, Jean Pierre Nourry, Didier Pasquier, Kathryn Gustafson, Renzo Bader. Also: Patrizia Falcone, Jaques Fiore, Peter Fleissig, George Katodrytis, David Kessler, Kate Linker, Marina Merson, Veronique Metadier, Raiwa Muderris, Jon Olsen, Mitsugo Osakawa, Don Paine, Nadia Petit, Patrick Winters, Pietr Zaborski

CONSULTANTS: Planning: Colin Fournier; Landscape: SETEC-TP; Interiors: Tschumi-Erhel Architects Associés; Structural: Peter Rice (RFR, Bridge & Gallery Structures), Hugh Dutton; Other Structures and Mechanical: SETEC-Batiment

Construction cost $300 million

**Supercrit #4: Parc de la Villette,
organised by EXP and supported by the
Architecture Foundation. Venue: Room
M421, Department of Architecture,
University of Westminster, 35
Marylebone Road, London, 14 October
2005. Presented by Bernard Tschumi.
Panel: Nigel Coates, Murray Fraser,
Peter Cook, Carlos Villanueva Brandt,
Bruce McLean. Chair: Paul Finch**

Samantha Hardingham   The Supercrit series focuses on architectural projects that stand out above others for their ability to catalyse the cultural preoccupations of a time – and sometimes a place – to open up questions of the usefulness of architecture beyond its purely formal obligations, and to review how theory in a variety of disciplines impacts upon design practice. Fundamental to the effectiveness of the series is for the architect or designer in question to present their project in person – putting forward a self-critical appraisal of the work, which in turn becomes a part of the project-making – and to a panel of critics who are selected on the basis of specific branches of knowledge relating to the project; contributing to the wider architectural and cultural context.

For Supercrit #4 we remain in Paris. Bernard Tschumi's Parc de la Villette was the next obvious choice to follow #3: The Pompidou Centre. Where Piano + Rogers' project set the tone and expectations for the Grand Projets, Parc de la Villette was one of its number. The Supercritics in this instance were: Peter Cook of Archigram and the UK's own architectural ambassador was invited to impart a first-hand knowledge of Tschumi's work since his arrival in the UK in the 1970s; Nigel Coates and Carlos Villanueva Brandt formerly of NATO (Narrative Architecture Today), both former students and then teaching partners of Tschumi's, were asked to comment on the legacy of the project in terms of subsequent design teaching; Murray Fraser of University of Westminster asked questions in relation to a wider architectural – and particularly theoretical – context; and artist Bruce McLean drew out the contrasts in the way artists and architects carry out and impact on each others' practice.

Parc de la Villette is another built project in the Supercrit series, but one that was a direct manifestation of both Tschumi's own writings and theorising on space, movement and event, and those of the wider architectural debate on deconstructivism, with which Tschumi was associated during the 1980s. Deconstructivism in architecture was influenced by deconstruction, the so-called school of philosophy and literary criticism named by French philosopher Jacques Derrida in the 1960s.[1] Deconstruction denotes a mode of analytical enquiry, meaning literally 'to undo' – to attempt to demonstrate that a text contains irreconcilable and contradictory meanings. Deconstructivism is not a direct application of this theory into architecture but is similarly characterised as 'challenging the very values of harmony, unity and stability [by proposing that] the flaws are intrinsic to the structure.'[2] These principles can also be directly linked to Russian Constructivism in the early 20th century where classical rules of composition were radically interrogated. In formal terms 'the deconstructive architect is not one who dismantles buildings, but one who locates the inherent dilemmas within buildings,'[3] applying strategies of fragmentation, dislocation and discontinuity into their design process. This shift in postmodern architectural thought and practice from neo-classicism to some kind of augmented constructivism was immortalised in an exhibition Deconstructivist Architecture at the Museum of Modern Art in 1988, curated by Philip Johnson and Mark Wigley and featuring the work of the movement's key exponents: Frank Gehry, Daniel Libeskind, Rem Koolhaas, Peter Eisenman, Zaha Hadid, Coop Himmelb(l)au and Bernard Tschumi. These architects, when listed together here, represent

1. Derrida's collaboration with Peter Eisenman on the design of one of the gardens in Parc de la Villette makes an explicit connection between this area of philosophy and architecture, although it may serve to inflate their affinities.

2. Mark Wigley, Deconstructivist Architecture (Museum of Modern Art, 1988), p 11.

3. Ibid.

what Wigley refers to as an 'uneasy alliance' – seven architects, all with quite different preoccupations, but whose interests overlap here for a brief moment in time. Built and unbuilt works on show included: The Gehry House, Santa Monica (1978–88), Libeskind's first-prize-winning entry for the City Edge competition, Berlin (1987) and Hadid's The Peak (1982). Tschumi earns his place with the Parc de la Villette; described as 'an elaborate essay in the deviation of ideal forms. It gains force by turning each distortion of an ideal form into a new ideal, which is then itself distorted … in this way, the park destabilizes pure architectural form.'

An architectural competition held in 1982 called for designs for a '21st century park' combining parkland, a Museum of Science and Industry, a City of Music, a Grande Halle for exhibitions and a rock concert hall. On a more societal note, President François Mitterrand stated at the time the fundamental challenge of the programme: 'We will have achieved nothing if in the next ten years we have not created the basis for an urban civilization.'[4] This particular competition called for 'open space for free-imaginings' in an area of northeast Paris created by Napoleon III in 1867, previously home to the abattoir and cattle market up until 1974. The 135-acre site spans the intersection of two canals: the Ourcq Canal and Saint-Denis Canal. Bernard Tschumi's winning entry was selected from nine finalists out of 471 entries overall – the only other architect in the nine was Rem Koolhaas alongside seven landscape architects. The jury was chaired by landscape architect Roberto Burle Marx and included Pierre Dauvergne, Vittoria Greggoti, Arata Isozaki and Renzo Piano. Tschumi's appointment (at the age of 39) was both as master-planner for the area, working with an expanded field of artists, designers and philosophers contributing to gardens and aforementioned buildings, and as designer of the Parc's key elements. He described his winning scheme as 'a large metropolitan venture, derived from the disjunctions and dissociations of our time. It attempts to propose a new urbanistic strategy … articulating concepts such as "superimposition," architectural "combination" and "cinematic" landscapes … the largest discontinuous building in the world.'[5]

Tschumi's own scheme is frequently described as a built diagram – as he explains more fully in the Supercrit – derived from previous theoretical work explored in the publication The Manhattan Transcripts and a diploma project set to students at the Architectural Association in 1976 entitled 'Joyce's Garden'. It tests ideas of an 'event' architecture. The three main organisational elements or 'systems' of the Parc are derived from the invention of a drawing that can talk about space and event simultaneously in architecture: the diagramming of captured film sequences – with the presence of human body movement as the activator of spaces – combined with points of intensification at the intersection of 'as found' and imagined programmatic scenarios. First, the point grid (tested previously in 'Joyce's Garden') was applied at the Parc, providing both a synthesising layout for the distribution of folies (meaning madness in French) at 120 metre intervals (that house 'point-like', i.e. activities such as a nursery, a kiosk, a nightclub that punctuate the plan at regular intervals) and a loose and discontinuous framework: on the one hand 'the single built common denominator' and on the other the folies themselves containing the very logic of 'dis-placements and dis-structuring'.[6] Second, the lines – a main

4. From a speech by François Mitterrand to the Public Construction Contractors' Professional Association, 1982.

5. Bernard Tschumi, Cinegramme Folie: Le Parc de La Villette (Princeton Architectural Press, 1987).

6. Bernard Tschumi, La Case Vide: La Villette 1985, exhibition at the Architectural Association, 20 February –2 March 1986. Review in 17 parts by Jacques Derrida, translated by Kate Linker.

coordinate system relating to linear activities of pedestrian movement along a North–South Passage between subway stations and the heart of the city, and the East–West Passage linking to the suburbs. The line system also incorporates the 'Path of Thematic Gardens' or 'Cinematic Promenade' – a curvilinear route through a series of garden 'sequences and frames' or 'cinegrams'. Finally, the surface system accommodates 'all activities requiring large expanses of horizontal space for play', varying in surface texture according to programmatic requirements: tarmac, grass, gravel. Tschumi's points, lines and surfaces are his walls, floors and windows.

The concept of divergence, displacement and dislocation is followed through in all built elements of the Parc. Peter Rice designed the galerie structures with Tschumi: 'I find the approach of Bernard Tschumi interesting because it questions all of the normal conventions one uses when designing steel structures … One provokes conflicts, searches for the most unstable solution and emphasises the assymetrical aspects rather than the symmetry which is characteristic of the more normal and conventional approach.'[7]

The very real closeness between the ideas being questioned intensively through teaching up against the ambiguities of practice from this early point in Tschumi's career is a prescient detail, both in terms of the broad ambition of this scheme, and the refreshingly direct nature by which drawings and diagrams become manifest on site. His humanistic understanding of the architect as a designer and skilled statesman who must operate at both micro and macro levels – simultaneously universal and particular in his concerns – is apparent in several of his later built projects. Like the Parc, projects such as Le Fresnoy Art Centre in France, Interface Flon in Lausanne and most recently, the New Acropolis Museum in Athens, all clearly read in relation to the city whilst possessing a strong sense of their own interior circulation and orientation – and are consequently photographed thus. Based on Tschumi's thesis that 'architecture can generate interaction' these schemes serve to facilitate a more coherent reading of previously lost or disconnected parts of the city. However, he does not seek to smooth over differences, but conversely opens up new routes and operational dialogues by way of generating a contemporary re-reading of the city. Perhaps this is where the influence of Cedric Price is most evident in Tschumi's work.[8] In a strictly metaphysical sense, they both see architecture as a means to liberate rather than to confine.

7. Peter Rice, An Engineer Imagines (ellipsis, 1994), pp 146–7.

8. 'Th[is] office tries, with varying degrees of success, to convert what is considered a healthy uncertainty, that is one which is not cowed by doubt, into delight in the unknown in relation to the operation and indeed the developing form of the eventual building.' Cedric Price, 'ECHOES – Environment Controlled Human Operational Enclosed Spaces', AD (October 1969).

PROJECT ILLUSTRATIONS

Perspective view of the North–South and East–West Galleries

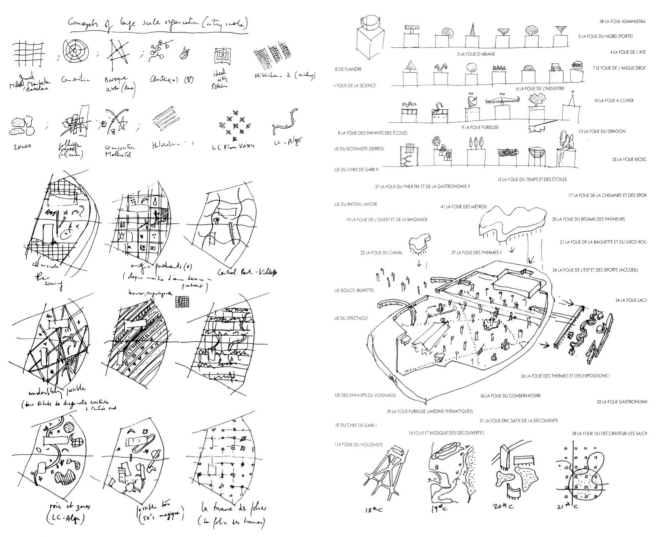

Variants of organisational diagrams

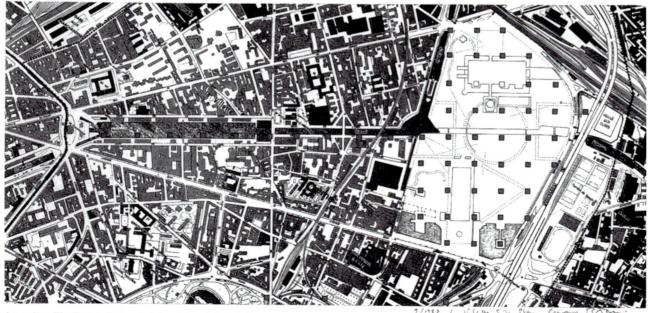

Area plan: 'The Parc forms part of the vision of the city'

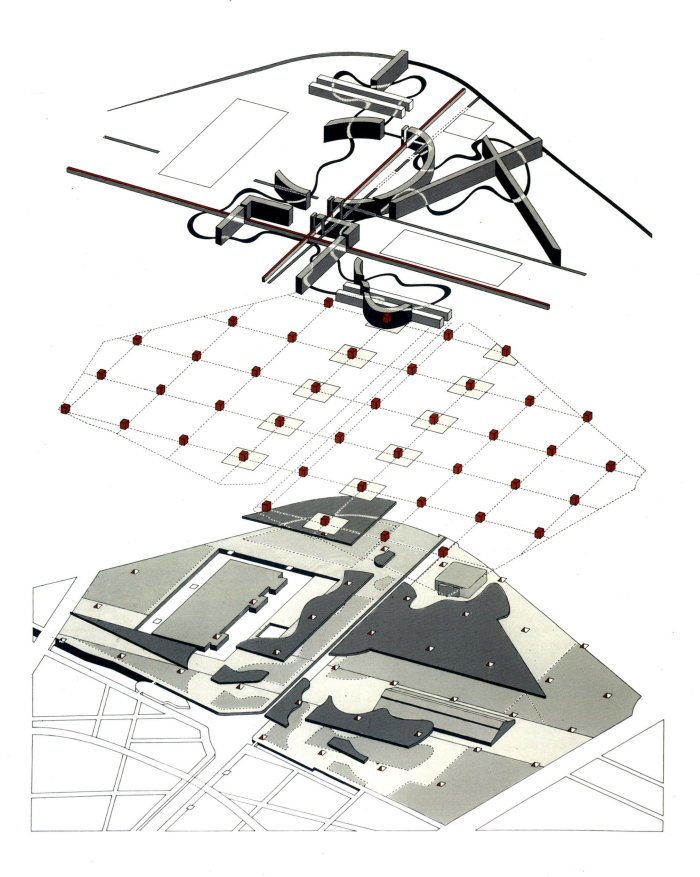

**Exploded axonometric revealing the
superimposition of points, lines and surfaces**

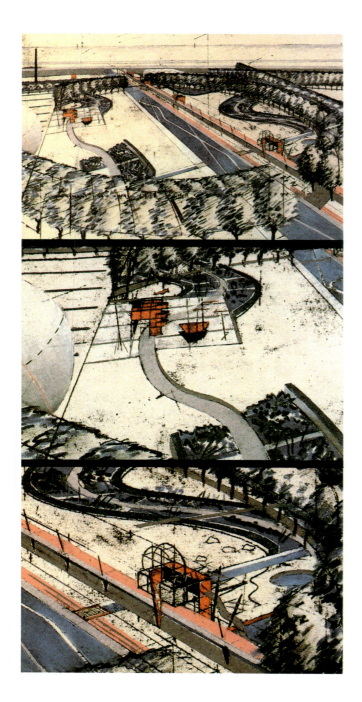

**Four illustrated series – in the manner of a
cinematic storyboard or film stills strip –
show sequences of potential movement
through and around various <u>folies</u>**

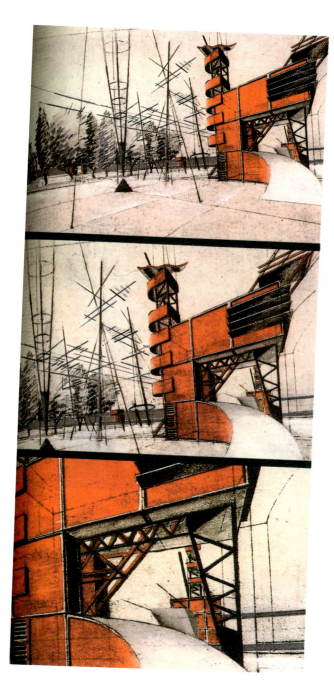 

Photograph showing the Parc in relation to centuries of building in Paris

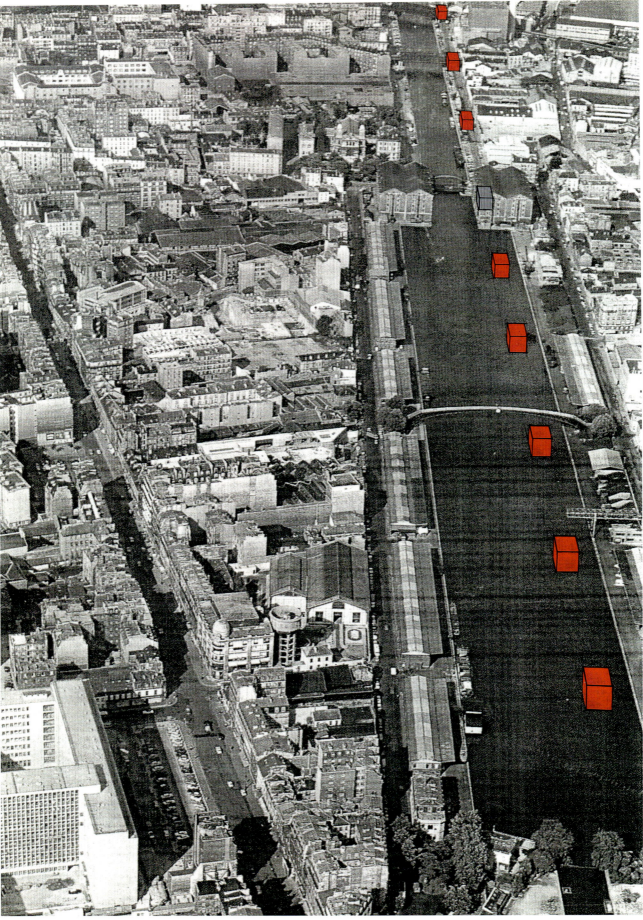

Aerial view collage: <u>folies</u> meet the canal

Photocollage of the notion of the Parc as part of the city

The fireworks display designed by Tschumi
for the opening night of the Parc in 1991.
Fireworks are a long-term preoccupation of
Tschumi's as part of his investigation into
devising a system of notation to describe
event action spaces. Fireworks make 'a point
about the pleasure of architecture and the
beauty of its uselessness' (taken from the
RCA exhibition Space: A Thousand Words,
and published as the first of Bernard
Tschumi's Architectural Manifestos in 1978)

EVENT HANDOUT

Supercrit#4: Parc de la Villette

Bernard Tschumi presents a proposal for an urban park for the 21ˢᵗ Century in Paris.

on

Friday 14ᵗʰ October 2005, 10am-12.30, in Rm.M421,
University of Westminster, 35 Marylebone Road, London NW1

SUPERCRITS

All architectural proposals go through some form of crit process, whether at college or in a client meeting. First there is the interim crit, then the final crit. Then there is the **SUPERCRIT**.

SUPERCRITS are a major international series, launched by **EXP**, the Research Centre for Experimental Practice, which puts projects that have "changed the weather" of architectural history back in the studio for expert and public critical debate.

Just as in student crits, we are asking the designers to present their project and discuss it with the panel of critics and the audience. **SUPERCRITS** are intended to allow you the audience to participate in the debate on some of the greatest projects of our time.

The panel of critics for Supercrit#4 will be:

Paul Finch (chair and editor of Architectural Review), **Peter Cook** (founder member of Archigram), **Nigel Coates** (founder member of NATO and head of the School of Architecture at the Royal College of Art), **Carlos Villanueva-Brandt** (founder member of NATO and unit master at the Architectural Association), **Bruce McLean** (artist) and **Murray Fraser** (University of Westminster).

OVERVIEW

The Parc de la Villette (1987) by Bernard Tschumi explores many of the ideas of Deconstruction, e.g. The attempt to separate the "signifier" from the "signified", or the form from its cultural meaning. It tests and develops ideas of Event Architecture – both architecture as an event in itself, and architecture as staging, responding to or being generated by the events around it. The park was one of President Mitterrand's Grands Projets which were built during the 1980's to regenerate Paris's role as cultural centre. The project was speculative, theoretical, polemical and until then had been seen as "paper architecture", designed for exhibition, publication and debate rather than to be built.

The project marks an end to the utopia of unity.

EXP would like to thank **Imran Patel** and **Call Print** for their generous support.

2

BACKGROUND

The Parc de la Villette was one of **the nine Grand Projets** launched by President Francois Mitterrand in 1981. The purpose of the grand plan was to *"announce the Paris of the year 2000"* with the intention of creating *"a new form of public facility...for a larger public, different kinds of people...for different forms of knowledge and for art. Beauty stimulates curiosity, responding to a need of the heart and the spirit."* Mitterrand stated the fundamental challenge of the program: *"We will have achieved nothing if in the next ten years we have not created the basis for an urban civilization."*[1]

The nine Grand Projets are primarily located along the main axis of the city, along the River Seine: **The New Ministry of Finance** by Paul Chemetov and Borja Huidobro, **The Bastille Opera** by Carlos Ott, **The Arab World Institute** by Jean Nouvel and Architecture Studio, **The Grand Louvre** by I.M. Pei, **The Orsay Museum** original building by Victor Laloux (1900), latterly converted by ACT Architecture. **The Arch at La Defense** by Johan Otto von Spreckelsen is west of the city to punctuate the historic axis along the Champs Elysees. The following projects were located in a group to the north east corner of Paris on the edge of the 19ᵗʰ century urban boundary: **The National Museum for Science, Technology and Industry** by Adrien Fainsilber, **The City of Music** by Christian de Portzamparc and **The Parc de la Villette** by Bernard Tschumi.

COMPETITION held in two rounds 1982-83.

Announced by Jack Lang, French Minister of Culture. The aim was to make Paris the arts centre of the world. Keywords were *pluralism* and *innovation*. The development would break with an industrial past and herald a new era of cultural super-abundance: *"open space for free imaginings"*.

471 entries in the first round 8 schemes selected for development for the second round. The jury was chaired by landscape architect Roberto Burle Marx and included Pierre Dauvergne, Vittorio Gregotti, Arata Isozaki and Renzo Piano. Bernard Tschumi, a French-Swiss architect aged 39 years old, won the compeition. Rem Koolhaas/OMA won second prize.

The architect describes his winning scheme as being conceived as *"a large metropolitan venture, derived from the disjunctions and dissociations of our time. It attempts to propose a new urbanistic strategy by articulating concepts such as 'superimposition', architectural 'combination' and 'cinematic landscapes'."*

SITE

[1] From speech by Francois Mitterrand to the Public Construction Contractors' Professional Association 1982.

3

Former home to the city's abattoir and cattle market (closed in 1974) covering 125 acres (one and a half times larger than the Tuileries Gardens) in the north-east corner of Paris. Located on a convergence of infrastructure: the centre of a residential area, close to the airport, international roads, two metro lines. The park is most notably defined by its waterways; the Ourcq Canal cuts the site horizontally in two, with Ledoux's Rotunda at one end of this axis. The St.Denis Canal runs down the west side of the park. The meeting point of the two waterways forms a canal roundabout.

BRIEF

Written largely by Francois Barre, managing director of the Etablissement public de la Villette, client and administrative body responsible for the park. The ambition was for *"a unique place of creation and invention, a common space for pleasure, invention and urban feeling"*, servicing the cultural needs of the city centre and facilities for the bordering suburbs. *"Action is favoured over objects"*.

Fuelled by the organizers' criticism of existing parks as *"repositories for children and old people"*. Parks in Paris during the 17ᵗʰ and 18ᵗʰ centuries played a more significant part in the social life of the city: as an urban place of encounter and interchange for adults, to hear news or look for amorous adventure - never just a garden but an accumulation of attractions. In the 19ᵗʰ century Haussmann (1852-71) realised the hierarchical system of squares, avenues, parks and woods. As the city grew denser with the onset of the Industrial Revolution the green spaces fulfilled other functions such as clean space for children and families. More recently the park or garden is now the green, a mere accompaniment to the buildings evoking neither the slightest emotion nor stimulating new activities – no pleasure.

The brief required that the symbolic dimension of the park be explored: the art of gardening, gardens reflecting a vision of the world and of capability, symbols and functions of the present to be incorporated into the contemporary park. A park of reconciliation: urbanism (man and the city), pleasure (body and mind), experimentation (knowledge and action).

Two spatial extremes: the garden city for activities and the garden in the city for relaxation.

The brief stated that it must definitely not be a
Post-modern garden: eclectic and nostalgic, but rather unified and coherent.

4

THE WINNING PROPOSAL

Tschumi claims the first *deconstruction* work was his own theoretical texts, *Manhattan Transcripts* (1976-81) which explore the concepts of superimposition and dissociation. The **Parc de la Villette** is the first *built* work to explore these themes. Tschumi describes the park as "the largest discontinuous building in the world".

Tschumi abandons the modern paradigm of architect as form-giver striving for unity and harmony and assumes that life is in fact neither harmonious nor consistent. He embarked on a strategy of differences and collisions in form and function. The approach is underpinned by a strong conceptual framework that in turn responds to the general unknowns in the project governing economic and ideological context.

A hybrid plan generates new activities and habits of use from unexpected encounters. A composition of three autonomous elements is superimposed on the site. **Points** (*folies*) are placed at 120 metre intervals as a common denominator for all events. Each *Folie* is essentially a 10X10X10 metre cube that can be transformed or elaborated. **Lines** (*routes*) form an orthogonal system of pedestrian movement, including the *cinematic promenade*. **Surfaces** (thematic gardens) for all activities requiring large expanses for horizontal play.

These built parts are designed *"to systematically produce dissociation in space and time"*. Useful to note the meaning of *folie* in its contemporary psychoanalytic sense as *madness*, e.g. the juxtaposition of unprecedented programs.

The parts function solely by colliding with a programmatic element such as the movement of bodies or the explosion of a firework. Thus elements of the program, budgets and priorities are interchangeable over time: a restaurant changes into a garden centre to arts workshop, whilst maintaining the park's overall identity.

Engineering teams: **RFR** - Peter Rice, Hugh Dutton, Henry Bardsley, Nadia Petit, Bernard Vaudeville (including Ian Ritchie and Jane Wernick) worked specifically on the Bridge and Gallery Structures. Also **SETEC-TP** and **SETEC-Batiment**.

Additional members of the design team included: Colin Fournier, Luca Merlini, Neil Porter, Steve McAdam, Kathryn Gustafson – see publication, *Cinegramme Folie* for full listing).

The following architects and landscape designers were involved in the project designing (although not all completing) gardens or additional greenhouses: Alexandre Chemetoff & Daniel Buren, Jean Nouvel, Hiroshi Hara, Peter Eiseman & Jacques Derrida, John Hejduk, Claes Oldenburg, Cedric Price, Kathryn Gustafson, Henri Gaudin, Gilles Vexlard.

5

Some questions:

- **Tschumi's question to himself:**
  "Is the Parc de la Villette a built theory or a theoretical building? Can the pragmatism of building practice be allied with the analytic rigour of concepts?"
  <u>*And his own answers:*</u>
  The project expanded in that it became better as difficulties increased, but was restricted in so far as La Villette had to be <u>built.</u>

- Is this a convincing architectural work because of or in spite of its awareness of other fields: literature, philosophy and film theory?

- Does the reversion to use classical axes to unify the plan resemble the Regency garden more than a vision of the 21st century?

- Tschumi's design is suited to involving many artists, architects, garden designers, industrial designers – is this possibly a true characteristic of the park of the 21st century.

- What did the competition reveal of the ideas current in contemporary park architecture and the attempts at innovation in designing the urban park?

- One cannot talk about La Villette without mention of philosopher, **Jacques Derrida**. What has his analysis of words, signs and ideas revealed to the architect about the building process, the built project and approach to future work?

- Undoubtedly humour in the project – which bit most delighted the architect?

6

Selected publications on Parc de la Villette:

Manhattan Transcripts, Bernard Tschumi, Academy Editions-St.Martin's Press 1981
Cinemagramme Folie: Le Parc de La Villette, Bernard Tschumi, Princeton Architectural Press 1987
La Case Vide, texts by Jacques Derrida, Anthony Vidler and Alvin Boyarsky, Folio VIII, Architectural Association 1986
Deconstruction, Omnibus volume, eds Andreas Papadakis, Catherine Cooke, Andrew Benjamin, Academy Editions 1989
Paris 1979-1989, Rizzoli 1988
Parc-Ville Villette, ed. Champ Vallon 1987
An Engineer Imagines, by Peter Rice, Artemis 1994
Designing Parks, Lodewijk Baljon, Architectura & Natura Press 1992
AA Files No.12, Summer 1986 (article by Jacques Derrida)
Architecture d'Aujourd'Hui, Feb 1983, Jun 84, Jun 89

PARTICIPANTS

1

2

3

4

5

6

7

8

9

10

1. Bernard Tschumi
2. Katharine Heron
3. Samantha Hardingham
4. Kester Rattenbury
5. Paul Finch
6. Nigel Coates
7. Murray Fraser
8. Peter Cook
9. Carlos Villanueva Brandt
10. Bruce McLean

Supercrit #4
Bernard Tschumi, Parc de la Villette
14 October 2005
EXP/University of Westminster
35 Marylebone Road, London

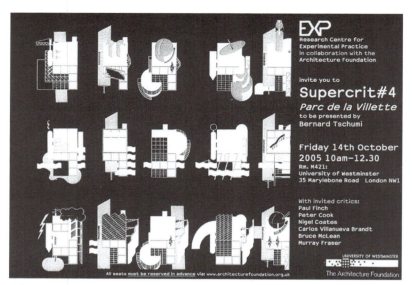

1. Poster for Supercrit #4

2. Piano + Rogers, Pompidou Centre, Paris, completed 1977 – subject of Supercrit #3

3. Various announcements that appeared in the French press around the time of the Parc competition

1. Narrative Architecture Today (NATO). A group founded in 1983 by Nigel Coates and included Mark Prizeman, Carlos Villanueva Brandt, Catrina Beevor, Robert Mull, Christina Norton, Melanie Sainsbury, Martin Benson and Peter Fleissig. The group formed in response to an end-of-year-assessment panel of Nigel Coates' Diploma 10 unit at the Architectural Association. External examiners of that year, James Stirling and Ed Jones, protested at the flamboyantly illustrative student work that showed no conventional working drawings. The then AA chairman Alvin Boyarsky encouraged Coates to take this opportunity to define the work more clearly. NATO ran for three years and published three issues of its magazine culminating in an exhibition of the work in 1985 at the Air Gallery, London.

2. The Grand Projets were civic building projects initiated by Socialist President François Mitterrand in the 1980s including, in addition to the Parc de la Villette, L'Institut des Finances (Paul Chemetov & Borja Huidobro, 1982), Musée d'Orsay (Gae Aulenti, 1987), L'Institut du Monde Arabe (Jean Nouvel, 1987), La Grande Arche de la Defense (John Otto von Sprecklesen, 1989), L'Opera de la Bastille (Carlos Ott, 1989), Le Grand Louvre (I.M. Pei, 1993), La Bibliothèque Nationale de France (Dominique Perrault, 1995).

3. Richard Meier (1934–), American architect, renowned for his pristine white modernist buildings, including the Smith House, Connecticut; the Getty Center, Los Angeles; and the High Museum of Art, Atlanta, Georgia. He was a central figure in the New York Five in the late 1960s (a group that also included Peter Eisenman, John Hejduk, Michael Graves and Charles Gwathmey), also known as New York Whites for their pursuit of a purist Neo-Corbusian architecture. See Peter Eisenman ed., Five Architects: Eisenman, Graves, Gwathmey, Hejduk, Meier (Oxford University Press, 1975).

4. Pun on the famous quote from architect Mies van der Rohe (1886–1969) 'Less is More'.

5. In 1961 the AA Council opened formal negotiations with the University of London regarding a possible merger with the Imperial College of Science and Technology (ICST). Regarded by consecutive AA Councils as a means by which future financial stability could be secured, AA members were balloted in 1964, voting in favour of adopting a Heads of Agreement drawn up with ICST. Negotiations stalled for several years but by 1969 a Declaration of Intent had been signed and a competition organised for the design of a new premises for the school. However, opposition from AA students and staff was very vocal, with the 'School Community' passing resolutions condemning the move which they regarded as eroding the AA's independence and removing their right to determine educational policy and practice. Disturbed by such demonstrations of internal disunity, the ICTS terminated negotiations in February 1970, stating that the basis for merger no longer existed. See Architectural Association, The AA and the Imperial College of Science and Technology, (1964) (Correspondence: AA Archives, 2006: S34).

6. Term coined by French philosopher Jacques Derrida in the 1960s in reference to contemporary philosophy, literary criticism and social sciences. Deconstructivism was the post-modern architectural movement in the 1980s which was influenced by Derrida's ideas.

Paul Finch   Welcome to the University of Westminster for Supercrit #4, Bernard Tschumi presenting the Parc de la Villette.**1** Thanks to EXP for arranging and the Architecture Foundation for co-organising this event.

Our distinguished panel of critics include: Nigel Coates, Head of Architecture at the Royal College of Art and co-founder of NATO;[1] Murray Fraser, Head of Diploma in Architecture at the University of Westminster; Peter Cook, co-founder and member of Archigram; Carlos Villanueva Brandt, co-founder of NATO and Diploma unit master at the Architectural Association; and finally artist and Professor of Fine Art at the Slade School of Art, Bruce McLean.

There has been a French flavour to this and the previous Supercrit where Richard Rogers talked about the Pompidou Centre.**2** Although not specifically one of the Grand Projets, the Pompidou Centre was a proto-Grand Projet for what was an extraordinary series of commissions from the French presidency partly to mark the Millennium, but also more importantly, to mark the 300th anniversary of the French Revolution.[2]

It was unprecedented for any country at that time to be so generous in the way that it used international competitions to find architects. And, although there were several French architects who won these Grand Projets, there were several won by outsiders. The jury for Opera de la Bastille, for instance, tried to second-guess the competition drawings by Carlos Ott – they thought they were getting Richard Meier.[3] Less, in this case, wasn't Meier.[4]

In 1984, I was editing Building Design, and a shockwave went through the office when this announcement came through: 'Tschumi wins La Villette'**3** – with that iconic three-layer drawing [See p 19]! It was an extraordinary year – the year that Zaha Hadid won the Hong Kong Peak competition.**4** That scheme wasn't achieved, but while the rest of us in our country were getting to grips with the fifth year of Margaret Thatcher as Prime Minister, inflation was in double digits, VAT had just gone up to 15 per cent, everything was in a bit of a mess – but, my God, on the architectural scene things were really buzzing.

In 1970–1 the Architectural Association School of Architecture (AA) underwent an educational experiment – deciding to stay independent rather than be taken over by Imperial College[5] – imperialism rarely works. Then suddenly, under the AA Chairman, Alvin Boyarsky,**5** there was this flowering of competition wins and this sense that ideas – and ideas that had come from outside architecture as well as from within it – could actually be translated into buildings and projects.

The La Villette proposal was new in being such a theoretically based project. Most of the country hadn't heard of deconstruction,[6] and many would probably have thought it had something to do with demolition. In a way it probably did have something to do with demolishing the notion that architecture could be perfect in the British context – which was of a civilised, polite, quiet modernism, with a little bit of neo-vernacular thrown in – and if you did it in brick almost anything could be satisfactory.

4. Zaha Hadid Architects, The Peak (Hong Kong, China), 1982–3

5. Alvin Boyarsky (1928–90), Chairman of the Architectural Association School of Architecture 1971–90. His legacy was a school that thrived on multiple and imaginative differences of approach and architectural preoccupation – both traditional and experimental – and at all levels of the school. His personal and spirited participation included on the one hand attending prospective student interviews, studio crits and portfolio reviews and on the other supported an emerging group of young architects such as Hadid, Tschumi and Libeskind marked by a particularly ardent period of exhibitions and publications in the 1980s

6. Robert Matthew Johnson-Marshall & Partners (RMJM), Hillingdon Civic Centre, completed 1976

7. Archigram office, 53 Endell Street, Covent Garden, London, c. 1972. Archigram secretary Lisa sitting with Bernard Tschumi reading Melody Maker and Colin Fournier looking through a camera with a student looking to camera (Credit: Kathy de Witt/RIBA)

7. Term applied to the international architectural movement with examples first cited in the late 1950s and early 1960s, though it did not come into common usage until the writings of Charles Jencks in the late 1970s.

8. Eidenossische Technische Hochschule, Zurich.

9. The 'AA jury' is the method of discursive critique, often with invited guests, that is conduced by the Architectural Association School of Architecture as a form of ongoing assessment and a system that has since been adopted by many other schools of architecture.

I think that view was summarised in Hillingdon Civic Centre[6] – a perfectly respectable, dull, end-of-the-road sort of building.

The other thing that was happening of course at the time was the whole question of postmodernism.[7] The explicit instruction in the competition brief was that this scheme was not to be a postmodernised park. Of course in a sense, even by that stage, everything was postmodernist. La Villette was one of those flowers or tendrils that sprang out of the ruins, or the demolition, of these old ideas. There was some universal modernism that was going to run the world forever.

I am going to ask Bernard Tschumi to re-present his project. Then we'll kick off a conversation and an opportunity to ask Bernard a whole load of – possibly impertinent – questions about the origins, themes and influences of La Villette. So, part crit, part conversation, part interrogation, and an opportunity to gather something from the people who actually did it!

Bernard Tschumi   It is highly intimidating to have a crit. I've never had a crit in my life. When I was a student at the ETH[8] in Zurich, we didn't have crits. We would put work up in a room by a certain hour in the afternoon. Then the teachers would lock the space and stay there alone for three days, leaving right at the end: C-minus! And that's all the exchange we would have with our teachers.

However, I do remember my first crit as a jury member at the AA.[9] It was quite fascinating. I had been invited by Peter Cook and I sat there for a whole afternoon.[7] Among other things, I remember that one student simply pinned up an old map of a part of north London, and nothing else, and the jury succeeded in saying extraordinarily intelligent things about that map for 20 minutes. Then they told the student that he had done great work, and the student went away.

So I thought maybe that is what I should do today. [Laughter as Bernard points to his site map; no other drawings are pinned up.]

I have to admit that, as a first-time jury member, I was petrified. I had never been on an AA jury before, so I said absolutely nothing during the first six projects. By the seventh, the last one in the afternoon, Peter said, 'Bernard, what do you think?' So then, under pressure, I said something and he hired me to teach.

I went on to teach at the AA for a number of years, first on my own, then with my former student, Nigel Coates. Then Carlos Villanueva Brandt came along, which was important because he enlarged the multinational aspect of the AA in the unit. And, because of my interest in the art scene and since so little was happening in the architecture scene, bringing in the artist Bruce McLean also had a lot to be said for.

In the mid-1970s, architecture rediscovered 'memory.' Almost everyone was into rediscovering 17th and 18th century artefacts and archetypes, or using them as starting points for projects. What this meant was that if you wanted to see something new, you had to look elsewhere – at

8. Nice Style – The World's First Pose Band (c. 1970)
(From left)
High up on a Baroque Palazzo (1974), Garage Gallery, London
Training shot, Hyde Park (1973), left to right: Robin Fletcher, Bruce McLean, Ron Carr, Gary Chitty, Paul Richards
Modified photograph featuring posing pole, Sonia Henie Niels Onstad Foundation, Oslo (1970)
Modified photograph from <u>Crease Crisis</u>, film (1973) – b/w, 23 mins

double level horizontal posing poles A & B pose 1. the slash   2 the glide

the art scene, in my case. Bruce McLean right here was the brain and gesticulating figure behind the group of performance artists – the original 'pose band' – called Nice Style,[8] who were using not only movement in very complex spatial constructs in a theatre mode, but also movement notations that, at the time, looked incredibly appealing to me as an architect. Their work brought up the idea of expressing movement in a drawing.

So, on one side, there was the new classical temple and the vernacular of the 18th century. On the other side, the idea that architecture is about movement in space. There was quite a gap.

9. Paris, May 1968: the student revolution and general strike in France that caused the eventual collapse of the de Gaulle government. On 3 May 300 students met at the Sorbonne University, initially in response to the closing of Nanterre University, but by later that day protests were joined by anti-Vietnam War campaigners and escalated into street battles. Protests and strikes by over ten million workers continued for over a month (Credit: Bruno Barbey/Magnum)

10. Philip Johnson, New York State Theater at Lincoln Center, 1964 – an example of New Formalism

11. Anton Furst, b. Anthony Francis Furst (1944–91), trained at the Royal College of Art. A distinguished production designer including sets for Stanley Kubrick's Full Metal Jacket (1987) and Awakenings (1990). He won an Oscar for his Gotham City and Batmobile for Tim Burton's Batman (1989)

12. Lutz Becker (1941–), filmmaker. Director of political and art documentaries such as Art in Revolution (1971) and more recently Century City (2001)

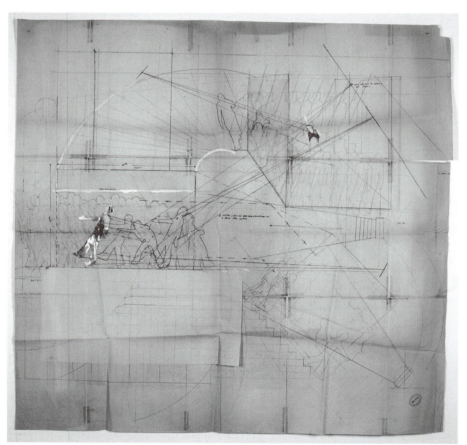

14. Sketch for The Final Pose Piece by Nice Style. The piece was photographed at Morton's Restaurant, Berkeley Square, London at 9.30 pm on 28 January 1975

10. New Formalism was developed between the mid-1950s and 1970s, combining monumental classicism with new materials and technologies of the International Style. Its key protagonists were Edward Durrell Stone (Music Center Campus, Los Angeles), Philip Johnson (The Lincoln Center, New York) and Minoru Yamasaki (World Trade Center buildings, New York). In the 1970s, the New York Five played an important role in articulating questions around the history and theory of the formalist discourse in architecture.

When the important international competitions started to take place in the early 1980s, a context had already been established for them during the previous few years. Here I would say that London was a crucial place – particularly at the AA, and perhaps because of something I have never seen anywhere else: students were asked to design their own programmes. A good professional is supposed to meet his client's needs. But at the AA you were asked to define those needs, and even to invent more than what the client might ever need or imagine.

Around that time, London had a particular climate that made it stand out in the architectural scene of the 1970s as an active, lively place. Most other places in the world had either collapsed or been stultified due to the 'explosion' of May 1968.[9] America was stuck in New Formalism,[10] [10] but in Europe – in France, Italy, and Austria – the old establishment had literally disappeared from view. Here in London, there were people like Cedric Price, Peter Cook and Archigram, who were capable of bringing a fresh view to things. So it was no surprise that Rem Koolhaas and Zaha Hadid, but also Daniel Libeskind, Leon Krier and a few others all found themselves in London. I think London was important as a climate that was relatively fresh and new – one in which, when you were starting out, you could establish your own work.

The La Villette competition was amazing – just to do a project, get first prize, and manage to get it built in the way you'd designed it. At the time, I had felt that architecture was not so much unbelievably corrupt as unbelievably discredited. Again, another London story: when I arrived in London, I had a friend from the Royal College of Art called Anthony Furst[11] who, together with a group of filmmakers like Lutz Becker,[12] was really interested in filmmaking and theatre. The first thing he told me was: 'Bernard, if you are in London, don't call yourself an architect; call yourself a designer. Architects have very bad press. Architects are always responsible for the little old lady who gets stuck on the 17th floor of her social housing tower block whenever the lift breaks down!'

So, the question in London at the time was really how to reinvent things. I embarked on a series of notations,[13] trying to see what 'architecture' might be. Imagine someone taking excerpts from film sequences and trying to map the movement of the protagonists onto those topical sequences. I used those arrows, those notations (which certainly owe something to Bruce McLean), to begin to see how they might have dynamic movement and could generate architecture.[14] In other words, you have something that comes from the movement of a body in space and not from the history of the 17th century. For four years I developed a series of diagrams, often inspired by B-movies and murder movies from different periods, largely the 1920s or 1950s, and developed a vocabulary and a definition of architecture that was not about facades, proportions and harmony (as one used to say), but rather about spaces, movement and events. I found it unbelievably powerful in terms of what architecture might be. In other words, it was a way of saying that architecture is both a space and about what happens in that space.

13. A sequence of notations from Tschumi's <u>The Manhattan Transcripts: Theoretical Projects</u>.
'Their explicit purpose is to transcribe things normally removed from conventional
architectural representation, namely the complex relationship between spaces and their use;
between the set and the script; between "type" and "program"; between objects and events.'
Scenes shown here are drawn from the films (top to bottom) <u>The Maltese Falcon</u>, <u>Psycho</u> and
<u>Screenplay</u>

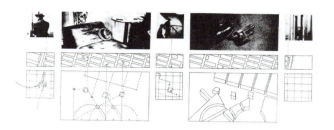

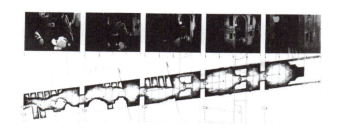

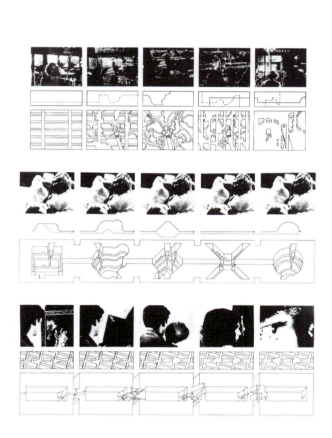

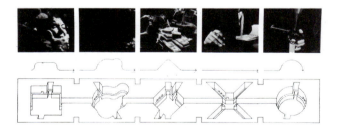

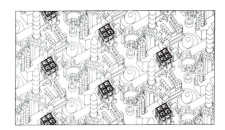

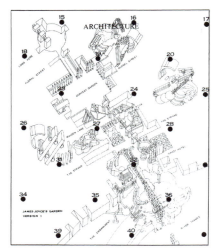

15. The 'Joyce's Garden' project was undertaken by diploma students at the AA in 1976–7. This is the project description, as cited in Giovanni Domiani ed., <u>Bernard Tschumi</u> (Rizzoli, 2003), p 40:

> The literary text, <u>Finnegan's Wake</u>, was used as the program for a project involving a dozen contributions by different students on a 'real' site, London's Covent Garden. The intersections of an ordinance survey grid became the locations of each architectural intervention, thereby accommodating a heterogeneous selection of buildings through the regular spacing of points. Moreover, the point grid functioned as a mediator between two mutually exclusive systems of words and stone, between the literary program and the architectural text. 'Joyce's Garden' in no way attempted to reconcile the disparities resulting from the superimposition of one text on another; it avoided synthesis, instead encouraging the opposed and often conflicting logics of the different systems. Indeed, the abstraction of the grid as an organizing device suggested the disjunction between an architectural signifier and its programmatic signified, between space and the use that is made of it. The point grid became the tool of an approach that argued, against functionalist doctrines, that there is no cause-and-effect relationship between the two terms of program and architecture.

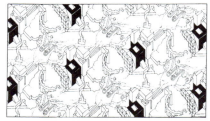

16. Site photographs show previous occupants: the 19th century Paris abattoir and meat market – 'Les Halles aux Boeuf, Le Marché aux Bestiaux et la Place de la Fontaine-aux-Lions, Paris'

17. Adrien Fainsilber, the City of Sciences and Industry, 1981. The Geode was designed by Fainsilber and Gérard Chamayou

11. Italo Calvino (1923–85), born in Cuba, was educated and lived from a young age in Italy thus becoming renowned as one of Italy's greatest fiction writers of the 20th century. He was a journalist, short story writer and novelist, recognised for surreal and allegorical fantasy stories such as <u>Cosmicomics</u> (1968) and <u>Invisible Cities</u> (1972).

12. Edgar Allan Poe (1809–49), American poet, critic and short story writer of deeply macabre works. His most famous poem <u>The Raven</u> (1845) epitomises the atmosphere of his writing. He is considered to be the father of the modern detective story.

13. Jorge Luis Borges (1899–1986), Argentine poet, short story writer and founder of several literary magazines. His works include <u>The Library of Babel</u> (1941) and anthologies such as <u>The Garden of Forking Paths</u> (1941, retitled <u>Ficciones</u> in 1944) and <u>Labyrinths</u> (1962). His writing is born out of an immersion in literature, philosophy, fact, fantasy and theology. At the age of nine he translated Oscar Wilde's <u>The Happy Prince</u> into Spanish.

After four years of doing this and having exhibitions in art galleries (which were the only places where this kind of work could be shown) and publishing my drawings and writings, I decided that I had a theoretical argument. Now came the time to try to test it out on a real competition, a real project – to test those arrows of movement, those movement vectors, and those points of intensities.

At the time, I had also done a project with my AA students called 'Joyce's Garden'.[15] It was during the academic year 1976–7. I had asked the students to take an excerpt of the text of Finnegan's Wake by James Joyce, which is obviously fairly complex in its manipulation of language, and make a project out of it. It wasn't the first time I had set such a brief; predecessors were texts by Italo Calvino,[11] Edgar Allan Poe[12] and Jorge Luis Borges.[13] The narrative was used as a way to replace the traditional programme, which tells the architect how many square metres for a living room or for a bathroom, for instance, and from which you have to design a plan. In this case, I was giving the students a short story, and the short story was the programme for the project. The hypothesis was that since the square metres of a programme are generally determined by cultural habits, why not start with culture itself, in this case, a literary text? 'Joyce's Garden' was actually too complex, and so a structure was invented – probably by Nigel Coates – based on a survey map and introducing a point-break over the site, which was Covent Garden. We put a point on a grid every 100 or so metres, in such a way that each student could take one of the points and make it into a project.

When the La Villette competition arrived, I thought I would test a number of hypotheses. The site[16] was about half a mile (800 metres) across and three-quarters of a mile (or 1 kilometre) from top to bottom. It was very much a site of industrial residues, of industrial archaeology. It still had abandoned slaughterhouses, but most of the buildings had been torn down. The grand halle or marketplace was still there – there had been a Rolling Stones concert in it not long before – and there was a large building that was intended to become a huge slaughterhouse that was being rehabilitated as the future Museum of Science.[17] But there was nothing to grab onto in order to start the project.

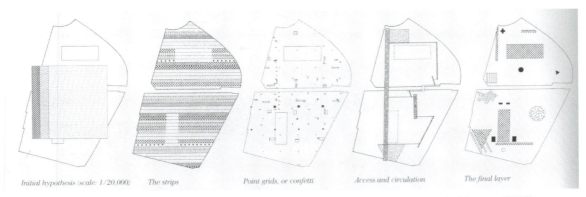

18. Rem Koolhaas/OMA, competition scheme for Parc de la Villette (Credit: Office for Metropolitan Architecture (OMA))

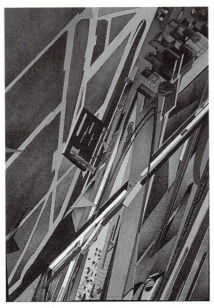

19. Zaha Hadid, competition scheme for Parc de la Villette

20. Le Corbusier's Plan Voisin (1925) for Paris envisioned a complete demolition of the north bank of the Seine to make way for 18 skyscrapers, greatly increasing the density of the area and by way of bringing Paris into the age of the skyscraper and the automobile

14. A French architectural and urban planning firm started in 1955 by Georges Candilis (b. Baku, Azerbaijan, 11 April 1913), Alexis Josic (b. Stari Becej, Serbia, 24 May 1921) and Shadrach Woods (b. New York, 30 June 1923; d. New York, 31 July 1973). In the 1950s Candilis and Woods were involved in finding housing solutions for the rapidly urbanising Islamic countries by combining low-cost prefabricated construction with traditional residential patterns. As members of CIAM, Candilis and Woods presented experimental housing units such as the Beehive Block (1952) and the Semiramis Block (1953) at CIAM IX (1953), where they proved influential in consolidating the ideas of TEAM X.

15. Colin Rowe and Fred Koetter, Collage City (MIT Press, 1984).

I started to test out a number of large-scale organisations, something that we've done in work over and over again since then. Whenever we start with a new project we look at all the different possible organisations; we test a few and then choose one to develop. Interestingly enough, one of our options for organising the site had a series of horizontal bands (like Rem Koolhaas's proposal for the same La Villette competition),[18] except that we turned the bands at a 45-degree angle. In another option, we had scratches going in all possible directions – that was not unlike Zaha Hadid's entry![19] And in another, we had something that looked like Leon Krier, because we knew that it represented the climate of the time. We chose the point-grid because it gave us an enormous amount of flexibility. It's important to remember that La Villette was designed as a master plan. In the beginning, I was not meant to build all of those red buildings [the folies]; I was just to be the chief of planning for the whole area and, if lucky, I might be given a small corner with a building on it to design. The fact that it was a master plan was one of the reasons I was able to be selected – considering I was someone who had never built anything before, who had practically never worked in an office (with the exception of ten months at Candilis-Josic-Woods in Paris[14]), and had absolutely no serious experience in how to put a building together. It's because it was, after all, nothing but a master plan.

But the project was actually quite complex. The site was the largest contiguous area to be designed within the historical confines of Paris; overall, it was 125 acres, or 55 hectares. The client had given us a programme that was 500 pages long, written by five different committees, none of whom were coordinating with one another. So for one committee, the Parc was about the old people in their wheelchairs, taking in the sunshine. For another, it was about the kids playing football. For yet another committee, it was about continuing the European city and the creation of urbanity. The amount of money that was being put into the state project and the political parties involved meant that no single body could control the whole thing. It's possible that the point-grid that I had used led everyone to think: 'Oh, we can do anything.' Anybody could read anything into it. But at the same time, it gave us, as the architects – and here I really shouldn't say this – incredible power to provide a common denominator for often-conflicting agendas among different political constituencies, users, and local inhabitants. So when I chose the point-grid, it was really as a strategy rather than as a project.

I also had an image in mind. A book by Colin Rowe called Collage City[15] was very important at the time. It was about the recreation of the 18th-century city, with its plaza, colonnades and streets. I hated that book. One specific diagram in it was presented as the epitome of 'the bad.' It was Le Corbusier's Plan Voisin in Paris,[20] a project based on a point-grid. The diagram was printed in juxtaposition with the wonderful city of Barcelona, or perhaps Madrid or Rome – I don't remember which one – showing the great plazas and streets. At La Villette I rejected this by stating that for the park of the 21st century, we were not going to return to the 17th century; instead, we were going to take a bit of the 20th century, but try to turn it into a model for a type of architecture or urban design for the 21st century. By this, I was also stating that it's not only a strategy, not only a park, but also an attitude.

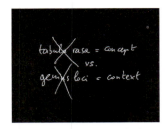

**21. Tabula rasa vs genius loci
(lecture slide)**

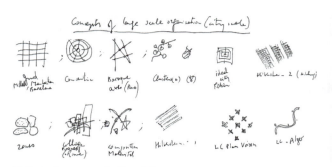

22. Variants on organisational diagrams

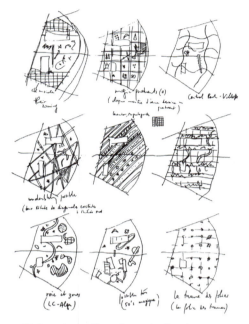

**23. Superimposition of organisational
diagrams onto site**

24. Arrangement of a regular and a random grid over the site

**26. The exploded axonometric
diagram shows the overlays of
'space', or the horizontal planes of
the Parc; 'event', or the points of
intensity and action; and 'movement',
or directions through the Parc. In a
sense a re-drawing of the notations
explored in The Manhattan
Transcripts**

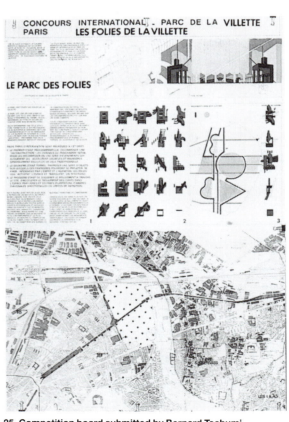

25. Competition board submitted by Bernard Tschumi

16. Excluding Tschumi and Koolhaas, the other competitors in the second stage of the competition were (in alphabetical order): Sven Ingvar Andersson, Andreu Arriola, Rich Bakker/Ank Bleeker, Alexandre Chemetoff, J. Gourvenec/J. P. Raynaud, Bernard Lassus, and Giles Vexlard/Laurence Vacherot.

17. Le Corbusier's Algiers Plan, entitled Plan Obus (1931–42) was generated in response to a government conference about the future city of Algiers – at that time heralded to become the world capital of Africa. Le Corbusier's disapproval of a French colonial scheme proposed by Henri Prost prompted him to travel extensively and work for 11 years on finding new forms for the city. His plan, a modernist mega-structure comprising a residential area, a waterfront business district and elevated highway, remains unbuilt.

There were 471 entries in the competition. It was my first competition for a real commission. The first stage had been anonymous, and the jury kept nine that were equally ranked in the second stage. Among these nine, there were only two architects – Rem Koolhaas/OMA and myself – and seven landscape architects.[16] Inevitably that created a major polemic, not only within architecture (where it is always good to discuss respective attitudes), but also among the landscape architects, who were furious; they are still mad at me today, some 25 years later. I was announced as the winner, and within about three years of unbelievable battles over the logic of the project, I found myself with an office of nearly 30 people, in charge of the design of the whole Parc. But that's another story.

Back to the crit. Let's look at some drawings. The sketches show the system of multiple strategies. The first one indicates the strategy of the points. Some parts of the Parc were simply neutralised – for example, the Museum of Science site and the area that became the City of Music – because I had no power over them. A series of sketches called 'Articulating a Concept for a Project' was produced because I thought, well, you don't start from scratch; you have a concept, a set of ideas, so you don't need to struggle with the programme. The concept involved a kind of tabula rasa approach, as opposed to following the genius loci or context.[21] Then there were organisational diagrams,[22] from the grid to the concentric circle, as found in the Baroque, in Le Corbusier's Plan Voisin, and in his plan for Algiers, Plan Obus.[17] While we all may invent things occasionally, most of the time these things have been around, in one form or another, for a long time. Then we superimposed each of those concepts onto the site itself,[23] laying out the strips à la OMA, and so forth. Finally we confronted the question of whether the grid would be a regular grid or a random grid.[24] Remembering the deep rationalism of French politicians, I decided that rationality would always win out, so I chose the regular grid.

Looking over the first three or four boards we submitted,[25] you can see how crude the production is when compared with today's competitions. The inflation of imagery by hyperrealist computer rendering has taken over today, as opposed to the diagrammatic drawing that tries to explain a concept.

One concept was the most important concept of all – the one that could articulate a definition of architecture. That idea came from a prior work, The Manhattan Transcripts, which is all about space, movement and event. The idea was that all the horizontal planes in the drawings could unfold in the Parc as spaces to be appropriated by future users; throughout them, there are points of intensity and points of actions, specific locations where things 'happen'. Finally, there are the movement vectors, which designate movement through and around the Parc.[26] The basic concept for the Parc, then, was the superimposition of points of intensity or events, a set of movement vectors (some very rigid, some extremely flexible and distended) and a set of planes. There were no constraints for the planes and I wouldn't design what would happen on them; this was not a park that was trying to recreate nature, but rather a piece of the city.

27. View along the canal

28. Intersection of bridge and <u>folie</u>

29. Luca Merlini, Swiss/French architect. Established merlini + ventura architects in 1997, he teaches and is the author of an architective (architecture + detective) novel, <u>Géographies de la Disparition</u> (Metispresses, 2009) and an urban novel <u>Les Habitants de la Lune</u> (Sens & Tonka, 1999)

30. Colin Fournier, architect (co-architect with Peter Cook of the Kunsthaus, Graz, 2003) and Professor at the Bartlett School of Architecture, University College London

31. Neil Porter, architect and partner of Gustafson Porter Landscape Architects, UK

32. Steve McAdam, architect and founder/director of the architecture and urban design practice, Fluid, UK

33. Peter Rice (1935–92), engineer. He joined Ove Arup & Partners in 1952 and went on to work on many notable projects including the Pompidou Centre, the Sydney Opera House, the Pyramid at the Louvre and Lloyd's of London

34. Hugh Dutton, architect and protégé of Peter Rice, helped on the structure of the covered galleries and bridges at La Villette

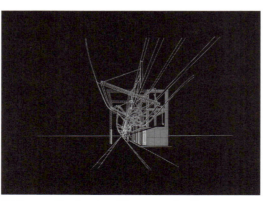

35. Perspective drawing of the covered walkway

18. Bernard Tschumi was Dean of the Graduate School of Architecture, Planning and Preservation at Columbia University, New York, from 1988 to 2003.

It was important that the three systems could be superimposed onto one another, while maintaining their internal logic. That was new. Throughout architectural history, I don't think there were many people (or, in fact, anyone) who had accepted that the logic of movement or the logic of space or activity – in other words, three autonomous, independent logics with nothing to do with one another – could be brought together as heterogeneous systems, rather than trying to coordinate, reconcile, or harmonise the different constraints of a building. The superimposition brought about extraordinary tension. The logic of each plane might be resolved internally, but the juxtaposition would result in something entirely different that took the action or event that occurred in space as an integral part of the architectural definition.

You can see some of these different logics at work in the buildings, the folies, which are always based on an identical frame – a red 12-metre by 12-metre cube – that is subjected to permutations and combinations and intersected by the different movement vectors. Diagonal ramps and vertical elevators or stairs cross through the building and intersect outside with the logic of movement, as expressed in bridges, covered walkways, paths,[27] jogging tracks, and so on, that articulates the motion of visitors through the Parc. You can see that here, where the folie is intersected by an elevated walkway[28] (I like this one a lot), or the curved garden promenade has a bridge. The logic of movement is thus always separate from, but intersecting with, the logic of space.

Here I want to mention the names of some people who were important to the development of the project during and after the competition phase. From the competition phase onward, there was Luca Merlini,[29] a young Ticino architect who had come to New York. After the competition phase, some key people are Colin Fournier,[30] Neil Porter[31] and Steve McAdam,[32] all of whom I met here in London. Colin, who first came to Paris to help me with the project contract, is still one of my dearest friends. As a planner and an urban thinker, he had more experience than I did, and he was also very, very good at dealing with politicians and thus played a key role in enabling us to build the damn thing. Neil Porter and Steve McAdam, then young graduates of the AA, both came to work on the early phases of the project, bringing talent and enthusiasm with them. Another person dear to my heart and also from London was the structural engineer Peter Rice.[33] An AA graduate, Hugh Dutton,[34] assisted him. Peter worked on the bridges and the covered walkways[35] – not the folies, which, in structural terms, are very simple buildings – and my conversations with him taught me a great deal about conceptualising structure. I remember that one day I invited him to speak at Columbia University[18] and he didn't have a title, so I gave him the title 'Unstable Structures'. He started his lecture by saying that no structure is ever unstable, and that the definition alone would get him thrown into jail. And then he argued for an hour about the notion of unstable artefacts! That is very much a part of what the Parc de la Villette is 'about'. It is constantly unstable. There are all sorts of different publics, different users, at all different times of the day or night. It is a constantly changing environment, no matter what the weather. It is also the only park in Paris that is un-gated and open 24-hours-a-day. (In Paris parks, you are usually not allowed to walk on the grass. I got that restriction overturned, too.)

36. La Villette: continuing the city fabric in a discontinuous way

37. Frederick Law Olmsted (1822–1903), landscape architect. His most celebrated designs include Mont Royal in Montreal (1876), the landscaping around the United States Capitol Hill in Washington DC (1874) and Central Park in New York (completed in 1873 with architect Calvert Vaux and shown here). The latter was proposed as the 'Greensward Plan', a naturalistic design, a complete work of landscape art and notable as an early example of the park as a public institution that had previously not been a prerequisite of all urban green spaces

38. Stourhead, Wiltshire, UK. The house, a Palladian mansion, designed by Colen Campbell (1720–4) and home of the Hoare family from 1717 (previously home of the Stourton family for 700 years). The gardens were designed by Henry Hoare II and laid out between 1741 and 1780 and are considered to be at the forefront of the 18th century English landscape movement that celebrated nature as inspired by the landscape painters of the 17th century such as Claude Lorrain (1600–82)

39. Vito Acconci, Step Piece, 1970. In this piece the artist 'stepped on and off a stool in his apartment every morning at the rate of thirty steps a minute, continuing the effort for as long as possible; the results of his "daily improvement" were distributed to the art public in the form of monthly progress reports'

40. Michel Foucault (1926–84), French philosopher, sociologist and historian. Published works include Madness and Civilization: A History of Insanity in the Age of Reason (1961) and The Order of Things: An Archaeology of the Human Sciences (1966) (Credit: Martine Franck/Magnum)

41. Jacques Derrida (1930–2004), French philosopher and founder of deconstruction. Major formative texts include Writing and Difference, Of Grammatology and Speech and Phenomena all published in 1967

42. Sergei Eisenstein (1898–1948), Soviet Russian film director and film theorist notable for his silent films, including Battleship Potemkin, Strike and October, and his use of montage in film-making, characterised by a 'collision' of shots denoting conflicts of social value, scale, volume, rhythm or speed (Credit: Eugene Robert Richee © Hulton-Deutsch Collection/Corbis)

43. Still image from film Battleship Potemkin (1925)

19. Sol LeWitt (1928–2007), American minimalist and conceptual artist, whose work focused on the cube and the square, working in a series of permutations.

For all their so-called 'sculptural' quality, the <u>folies</u> are not abstract sculptures in the manner of a Sol LeWitt[19] artwork or even a Richard Meier building. They are about the dialogue between contemporary buildings and the reality of the city. This is most apparent in the drawing that shows the grid of <u>folies</u> extending out from the city of Paris as a repetitive and potentially unending succession of buildings.[36] La Villette's explicit status as an 'urban' park also contrasts with the paradigm of Olmsted[37] or of the English park[38] as a replica of nature. Despite their green grass and somewhat eccentrically planted gardens, the flat surfaces of the planes are not programmed; I didn't and do not design what happens on them. For example, during summer nights, the large green field at the centre of the Parc becomes a 3,000-seat outdoor cinema theatre. This is what I mean when I say that La Villette is a piece of the city, a variegated space of cultural places. It is a new type of park – a park of 'culture,' not 'nature'. But the Parc is also more broadly 'cultural' in the sense that its design was informed by some of the ideas of the day. I mentioned earlier that I had been fascinated by the work of artists like Nice Style. I should also mention Vito Acconci and other American artists who were interested in the interaction of the body with space.[39] In the art field, but also in the literary world, I found others who were asking the same questions as I was, in totally different ways. At the time I knew as much about art, cinema and literature as I did about architecture. I had read people like Foucault,[40] who discussed the circulation of power and the establishment of archetypes like prisons and hospitals, but also people who were asking questions about the notion of stability, the notion of 'truth', and what were, at the time, very radical questions about our society.

One of them was Jacques Derrida.[41] We should get one thing straight here: the Parc was hardly inspired by his theories. I do not think you can 'build' deconstruction. Derrida was more of an ally, in the same sense that I was looking for people to support and confirm what I was doing in certain 1920s work, like the films of Sergei Eisenstein[42] such as <u>Battleship Potemkin</u>,[43] and the work of the Dadaists,[44] Surrealists,[45] and Constructivists.[46] I thought Derrida was asking many of the same questions about foundations and fundamental concepts in his field that I was asking myself in architecture. So I invited him to come and design a garden at La Villette, and I paired him with Peter Eisenman.[47] He had never been approached by an architect before. When I first asked Derrida to come to my office, he immediately asked me: 'Why are you interested in deconstruction? Because deconstruction is anti-form, anti-hierarchy and anti-structure.' My answer was: 'Precisely for those reasons!'

At the time, this pairing-up caught fire and everybody talked about it, but what was more important was that it demonstrated a wish not to accept all the received ideas about what architecture is. Architecture always needs to re-examine itself inventively. The La Villette project was not so much about how to condition design, but rather about how to design conditions, namely, to try to stage situations, specifically urban situations. Right now there is a lot of discussion about the idea of surfaces, and conditioning the package or packaging of architecture. But the intention of my project was much more about designing the conditions that can

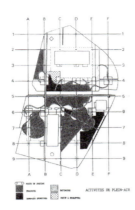

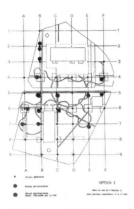

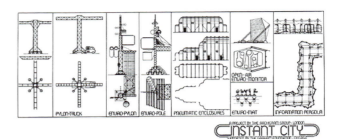

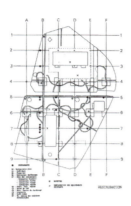

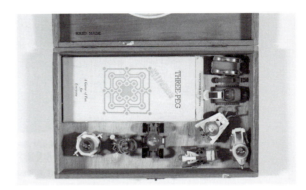

48. 'Extreme rigidity is wonderful'

49. Archigram's Instant City (1968) demonstrates the group's 'kit-of-parts' design approach (Credit: Archigram/Archigram Archives)

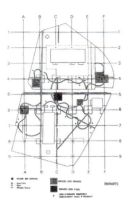

52. Anni Albers, wall hanging, 1927 (Credit: Picture Scala, Florence/MoMA)

50. Cedric Price frequently employed toys and games to derive his 'kit-of-parts' design logic. Shown here (as found stored in a customary cigar box) are a family of small plastic interchangeable vehicles which are likely to have been used in his MAGNET project (1999) which proposed a series of short-life structures for London. Also, a peg game which is stamped with GENERATOR (1976), a single storey office building, made up of a number of relocatable rooms and open corridors. The game was used to play out possible scenarios of movement and reconfiguration over time

53. Computer drawings of variations on folies. Computer drawing in architecture was in its early phases at this time

51. 'Erector Set' – 'loads of fun and constructive too!' – as advertised in an American boy's magazine of the 1950s such as Boy's Life

21. The term 'kit-of-parts' in architecture commonly refers to a design process that took up a modular, component-based approach to construction inspired by prefabrication techniques employed in the aircraft, automobile and shipbuilding industries.

Bernard Tschumi   This is a question by an architect who knows that we all have to struggle and strategise! I will tell you what works best and what doesn't work so well. Extreme rigidity is wonderful. Here it is at La Villette – an axis that is literally one kilometre long and just cuts straight through the project with authority.[48] Easy! Everybody understands that once you get the engineers rolling, you can have real production; you get a price, and so on. Then, in contrast, you have the circles [Indicates on drawing], and that is trickier because while they look rigid on the plan, they are actually made out of 75-year-old trees. So we had to bring fully grown trees into this deserted area. In another part of the Parc we had several formal promenades. That also was relatively easy; everyone could understand that. Then we had a meandering promenade that I called the 'Cinematic Promenade' [Indicates on drawing] because it was designed in analogy to the frames of a film. It was a series of sequences where we could invite people, mostly landscape architects but also artists and architects, to design gardens. The fact that it was meandering and had no rational logic meant that we could move it all the time. Isn't that wonderful – to be able to move things around and 'listen' to your plan!

But it proved to be unbelievably difficult, because the clients indeed wanted to change it all the time. They were always adding a bit here and a bit there – a riding club, a restaurant – and then we always had to move the promenade around. People were proposing different types of plans and different types of ground cover because they knew it could be moved. That is the second thing that can happen with the original idea.

Remember that I had never built anything, and I wanted a clear concept that I could explain easily and a project that I could develop with my team. We never worked with an associate or local architect – we did everything on our own and with a design staff that was relatively inexperienced in building. So for the buildings we decided to prepare a 'kit-of-parts'[21] – you remember the expression: it's Archigram,[49] it's Cedric Price.[50] Some were designed with a staircase, some with a ramp, or with certain sizes of rooms. That way we could have any configuration we wanted, as with Fisher-Price or an 'Erector Set'.[51]

Of course, we also looked at past precedents – for instance, the Constructivists and the Bauhaus[52] – to develop a vocabulary that could be the object of as many permutations and transformations as possible. For the first five or six folies, we developed a structural system, a cladding system, and the general concept of additive elements so that we'd have a clear logic in how to build them, how to price them. By number 21 or 22, we were able to produce a folie in two weeks, starting from the first sketch and programme.[53] Obviously, having computers, which became part of the process only later, helped speed things up.

In other words, I distinguish between these three approaches – the rigid approach, the one that is perfectly flexible and a complete headache, but wonderful, and the 'kit-of-parts' that allows you to have multiple configurations. One particularity is that the multiple configurations are also a function of experience: by number 22 we were happy, but we often struggled until then.

54. Frederick Olmsted, Central Park, completed 1873:
700 acres (280 ha) 'keeping the city out of the park'

55. Bernard Tschumi Architects with Derek Revington and others,
Downsview Park, Toronto, competition design proposal, 1999

22. Derek Revington, now an Assistant
Professor at the University of Waterloo in
Canada, is the architect of 'Luminous Veil',
part of the Prince Edward Viaduct System.

Paul Finch   Does that answer it Nigel?

Nigel Coates   Not completely, but maybe we'll come back to it.

Murray Fraser   I think the reason why I've been asked to be on the jury is that I have absolutely nothing to do with the Architectural Association, so I am very much the outsider on the panel. But, for somebody like myself who was finishing my architectural education around the time that this project was being realised, I am fascinated – largely because we had read a lot of AA theorists and this was the first time their ideas were to be tested as a real building on a major project – so I think that is why it had such resonance.

There are many things I'd like to ask, but one is about a general cultural reading on this kind of project, which is this notion of taking the values of the city, the urban city, into the park. You had written critically about Olmsted in Central Park trying very much to keep the city out of the park,[54] to have the park as something very different from the city. But this was an attempt, shall we say, to superimpose those sorts of value systems together, it seemed to me. It's a very powerful idea, and I remember it becoming a trope in many, many subsequent projects. I am beginning to wonder now, in retrospect, whether perhaps it was an overstated polemical point of the time and whether it still stands up as a strategy. Here it would be useful if you could maybe compare it with your entry for the Downsview Park competition in Toronto,[55] which you did a few years ago, and which if I read it correctly is much more fluid, much more about getting to the qualities of a park, of the natural landscaping, and emphasising that rather than the urban as in the scheme for La Villette.

Bernard Tschumi   After La Villette was completed I didn't want to have anything to do with a park again. I thought: 'I can't get back the circumstances, whether political or personal, that made that project happen.' I did, and still do, think that I can't upstage myself on that scheme, that park. So while I was receiving all sorts of requests to participate in other park competitions, or to be a consultant on other parks, I've always refused to this day – with one exception. An ex-student of mine from London, Derek Revington,[22] was living in Toronto. One day he called and said: 'There's this new park over here.' And I told him: 'I will never do a park again – that's it, done that.' And he insisted and insisted, so eventually I said I would do it, on one condition: I would try to take every concept, every idea, every word of La Villette, find its opposite, and then use those opposites as my new programme and see what happened. So, where at La Villette we talked about discontinuity, at Downsview in Toronto we talked about fluidity and continuity; where we talked about disassociation at La Villette, at Downsview we talked about merging into one another; where we talked about hardware at La Villette, at Downsview we talked about software; where we had points at La Villette, we had fields at Downsview; and so on. There was a list of about 13 names or categories. We did a project that I found extremely interesting in terms of doing opposites, but it was largely a mental exercise.

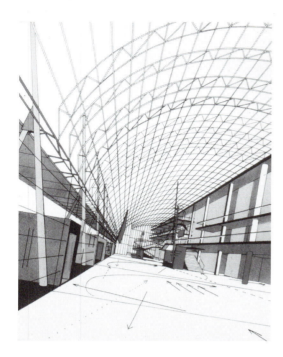

56. Bernard Tschumi Architects, the New National Theatre and Opera House, Tokyo, Japan, 1986, competition drawings. Two concert halls, an experimental theatre, rehearsal spaces, restaurants and exhibition spaces as well as dressing, loading and storage facilities

57. Bernard Tschumi Architects with Luca Merlini, Interface Flon, Lausanne, Switzerland, 1988–2001. An interchange of regional trains, a bus station and subway station, also serves to link parts of the city – by means of inhabited bridges – that were previously disconnected due to the dramatic shifts in topography across the site

58. Bernard Tschumi Architects, Le Fresnoy Arts Centre, Tourcoing, France, 1992–8. A centre for multi-media art, the building includes an umbrella-like canopy constructed over existing buildings, forming 'a succession of boxes inside a box'

23. Arata Isozaki (1931–), Japanese architect who studied and worked under Kenzo Tange before developing a strong Mannerist style in his own designs. Works include the Museum of Contemporary Art, Los Angeles (1981) and Team Disney Building, Florida (1989). Isozaki was also a member of the Parc de la Villette jury panel.

Paul Finch   But was it more of a mental exercise than doing La Villette? I mean, if they are flip sides of the same coin, aren't both these things experiments? Do you feel more profoundly about one or the other?

Bernard Tschumi   This is actually a profound question. Do you do competitions because you want to win them? Ask yourself. In the case of La Villette, I had told myself I wanted to do it both in order to win and to leave a mark on history, but frankly I had never thought that I would win. It was a bit like winning the lottery. No, what happens in a number of competitions, whether you are experienced or starting out, is that you do them in order to test certain things, to see how far you can push ideas one way or another. But then you win, and have the shock of winning! I don't know if I was that happy about the idea of winning La Villette – I was already really comfortable doing my own thing, and suddenly I had to open a real office. Once you are confronted with the fact of having to build your project, then the real work begins. That's when you have to 'materialise' the concept, since architecture does not exist without the materialisation of the concept, which allows the concept to evolve further. I really don't like it when I hear architects say: 'Oh, we wanted to do that, but then the client or a contractor made us compromise.' On the contrary, constraints or pressures are what allow you, or force you, to be far more precise about your priorities and what you want to do, and therefore to make a better building. So I'm sure if we had won the Toronto competition, we would have worked hard to make it a great project.

Paul Finch   This is an interesting point about an architecture which starts off by defining itself by its constraints – you know you can't do that, so you'll have to do that – whereas at La Villette it seems to me that you were in a position of saying: 'We're going to do this because of things that we want to do and it's not about constraints from the 17th or 18th century, or the planning authorities or even one or two of those multi-headed clients.' You took the things that you wanted to take and made a very proactive project, rather than a reactive one.

Peter Cook   I am interested in Bernard and his La Villette win as a life example. I can remember too (without being over nostalgic) that amazing event; Bernard won La Villette and Zaha won the Peak and we said: 'God, the breakthrough has happened!'

The key thing that Bernard represents for me is his amazing clarity. I'd like to mention some other competition projects by him, not necessarily winning ones. One is the National Theatre competition in Japan,**56** where I think he came third, and Arata Isozaki[23] told me that there was no way he could have won it, because the jury was determined a Japanese should win. But nonetheless that design with the striation of different activities was absolutely wonderful. Then there was the valley in his hometown, which he obviously knows like the back of his hand, and he bridged that valley several times with such a brilliant stroke.**57** Also, at Le Fresnoy, near Lille, where he did the building above the building.**58** It is an absolutely brilliant concept and made one think again about interstitial space as urbanism. And he keeps doing it! We were together less than a week

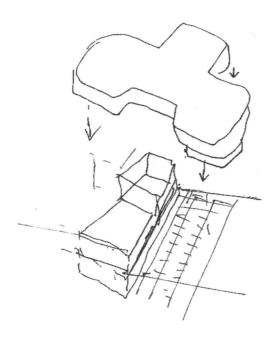

59. Bernard Tschumi Architects, Busan Multi-Media Cinema Centre, Busan, South Korea: International Competition entry, 2005. A complex of film theatres, visual arts centre and public concourse dedicated to film culture

technical studies TS6A

Prof Peter Cook
Cheerful Architecture

13th Oct 6.30pm Room M421

University of Westminster   35 Marylebone Rd London NW1 5LS
Baker Street Tube Station Buses 2 13 18 27 30 74 82 113 139 189 274

http://marylebone.wmin.ac.uk/silverp/technicalstudies.asp
Room M501 ext 3194 silverp@wmin.ac.uk   w.f.mclean@wmin.ac.uk

60. Lecture poster announcing Peter Cook's talk entitled 'Cheerful Architecture' delivered at the University of Westminster on the night before Supercrit #4

61. The Nestlé Headquarters in Vevey, Switzerland is one of the best-known works by Bernard's father, Jean Tschumi (1904–62)

ago in another place, a long way from here [in South Korea], where the clarity of his project [for the Cinema Centre[59]] was stunning, and the conversation with the jury afterwards was that Bernard is clearly the guy that understands film.

I'm going to be very naughty here and say that what strikes me about that project in South Korea, which I did briefly show in this room last night,[60] is that Bernard returns to some of the architectural principles of his father and in a curious way – this is very difficult for him. [Tschumi winces and hides in red scarf – laughter]. It has overtones of the Nestlé building[61] and its organisation. What was fascinating was that he did not go to his father's school, but to the rival school – the ETH – and had to speak another language. It occurs to me that Bernard later escaped to England largely because of Cedric Price, rather than sticking around Paris, which was too close for comfort. He came in the early 1970s and taught at Portsmouth Polytechnic, which is a difficult thing to do at the best of times, and then found some friends at the AA and the rest is history. In other words he made a number of leaps of escape, but the escape gave him the clarity to return to what he probably knew about.

The point about being attracted to Derrida because of anti-form and anti-structure to me is a paradox. What Bernard has actually done in his architecture is to redefine form and it serves me to be highly concerned about structure. There is another aspect to the work, which is after a certain condition of that Englishness that he came into, as when I think about Cedric's work, I think about an aspect that is brushed under the carpet at the moment – an element of the English picturesque, the English naughtiness, the English aside, the funny little narrative, which must have been one of the aspects that attracted Bernard, perhaps not consciously or intellectually, but was there as a constituent of the thing that was not in Paris but was in London.

There is also that thing in Rowe's interpretation which caused Bernard irritation: that in order to do something positive you have to have something that you really don't want to do. To have an anti-body sitting there irritating the hell out of you, so that you can leap over it – it is very important. So I think there is this type of tightness, looseness.

Something that has not been mentioned this morning is that Bernard cleverly – both abstractedly and with love I suspect – used the constructivist model for the objects. But constructivism was always there as a sort of thing that certainly the English would never do, or couldn't do. The question that this raises about materiality and surface is fascinating. I have an irritation of my own that not only do the English not like master plans but also they are bewitched by surface (and in a sense I can't even escape it myself). Whereas Bernard, as a multi-cultural person, is the intellectual, mental and physical bridge who is able to both love and hate certain things in his culture.

I can remember one day, Bernard took me round La Villette. It was clear that having established this very basic system (and the semi-abstracted part of me was satisfied by the need for architecture for the moment), that in a

62. Jean Nouvel (1945–), architect, was assistant to Claude Parent and Paul Virilio (1967–70), won the competition for the Arab World Institute, Paris, in 1981 and is currently completing his first building in the UK, One New Change, London (2003–11)

63. Bernard Tschumi pictured here with his father, architect Jean Tschumi (1904–62)

way the other people who were then brought in to do various bits of park or little bits of vegetation were a sort of mulch. And I remember Bernard saying: 'Oh, I've got this guy over there doing something in the corner, he's a bit vulgar sometimes but he is sort of interesting – and a bloke called Nouvel[62] – he's all right.'

What was so clear this morning is that Bernard is such a clear thinker and a clear teacher, that he is able to handle priorities and by doing that clears the decks for hiding the paradoxes. So, I suppose it is our task as critics (although we are not really critics) to winkle out the paradoxes.

Bernard Tschumi   There are not many people I would let try to psychoanalyse me. Unfortunately, there are at least two in this room today, so this is tricky. So I will continue the prior conversation that Peter initiated right now. First, talking about that particular project when you, sir, bring my father into it. My father was indeed an architect.[63] He died before I started to study architecture, and I have a lot of respect for the work that he did. I like it a lot, but it is quite different from what I do. That competition was for a large cinema centre in a large city in South Korea. We worked on it for a couple of weeks. And, as is common in competitions, we started to analyse the situation, looking at all the possible alternative strategies, and we decided on what we were going to do and began working on a very vertical, tall building. Then we found out that one of the other competitors had a pretty similar section. And so, exactly a week before the submission date, just as we had started work on the envelope, the surface, and so on, I was feeling a little uncomfortable. There's something very interesting about projects: whether you are a student or a really experienced practitioner, when you start a project you are working <u>for</u> the project. You are struggling, really trying, to get it right. But then a magic moment arrives when it turns around 180 degrees, and the project starts to work for <u>you</u>. And that vertical, tower-like building – it just wasn't working for us.

I woke up on that Friday morning at 3 am and thought, I'd better get up. So there I am, and I start, interestingly enough, to write a few words, trying to say what we wanted to say. By half a page down I had already done an entirely new sketch of the project. So we changed the project. We started from scratch exactly a week before submission. I walked into the office that morning at 9 am and six people couldn't believe their eyes. 'OK: throw it away, we're starting again, and this is what we're going to do.' We had to submit the following Friday at noon. So that explains the rough nature of the scheme. But then when I asked myself whether I would do that concept again, I said: 'Yes, I would do that concept again, because that was the right way to go about it.'

Questions of vocabulary and image (and now you <u>are</u> psychoanalysing me). There were two dimensions to the cinema centre project, one of which had to do with a sort of double envelope, which is a common thing these days. The other element that emerged was an almost complete symmetry that acts as a sort of hub. Now, does it correspond to particular things in my life? Here I'm going to become Bernard Tschumi again, theorising practice (which is a very important expression). That is, I believe that

64. Bernard Tschumi Architects, Paul L. Cejas School of Architecture, Miami, 2003

24. Le Corbusier refers to 'architectural promenade' in his work as an architecture built around a series of unfolding views – a choreography of space in tune with movements of the body.

25. A preoccupation in the work of architect Louis Kahn is the notion of servant spaces (e.g. vents, elevators, stairwells, corridors) and served spaces (main rooms such as offices or laboratories) and creating a clear formal distinction between the two spatial typologies.

26. See Carlos Villanueva Brandt, 'The Psyche of the Unit Master' in Paul Davies and Torsten Schmiedeknecht eds, An Architect's Guide to Fame (Architectural Press, 2005).

sometimes you touch upon things that you can pinpoint in history, including concerning your own father. Equally, there are certain concepts that are 'there' in architecture, often in key moments, whether you want them or not. Let me give you an example. Le Corbusier's 'promenade architecturale':[24] sure, it's one man's vision, but at the same time, it's now a part of our vocabulary. Or Louis Kahn and his ideas of servant and served spaces[25] – these, too, are part of those concepts of architecture. I'm really interested in these things because they are not about form or about what architecture looks like, but about what it does. So in this respect, I think that, for me, every time, the design concept will come <u>before</u> the form.

Paul Finch   It's the heroic retreat from formalism!

Carlos Villanueva Brandt   First of all I'll say something outside the crit, which is basically that I think the project is seminal. Surprisingly enough, it is not strange to be here as I have quoted this project in Diploma 10 introductions for so many years now that it is ingrained. The unit that Bernard taught at the AA continues and has continued on through Nigel [Coates] to myself. I show this project relatively often, I talk about it, and I've just written an article in a book[26] in which I mention this teaching tradition.

I think to a certain point, a) from the complexity of the project – what you are trying to do with the events spaces, and b) from the respect to do with culture, that I think your work is very cultural. It's interesting that you talk about the B-movies and the <u>Manhattan Transcripts</u>, which were fantastically influential too. Now in those projects you had control of the culture. The <u>Transcripts</u> are very nice because you are controlling them with the story, then they have a product at the end that is maybe not as good as La Villette – lets put it that way, from a critical point of view. So what seems interesting to me is in terms of the crit, how did you set up the testing mechanism for actually making the grid work? Because when you were dealing with the <u>Transcripts</u>, you were in control; there was a story there. When you were doing 'Joyce's Garden', there were narratives there. All of a sudden, in a way [in La Villette], you were in a formal world where you were saying that if certain layers came together something would happen. Now what I find interesting about that, what is so strong about that diagram, is that the city is involved in the Parc – it's a fantastic diagram. And you were obviously trying to do that in 'Joyce's Garden', but in the Parc it is rather restrictive because the field, or rather the landscape, doesn't have as much quantitative culture as the city. So I would like to ask you how you tested it when you did the project – and I think if you did test it, then it would be a very good diploma project, as it were – and, how you feel about the later projects, whether it is the Miami school**64** or Fresnoy, in which you also managed to do this layering, where you were using existing city fabric underneath, or in Miami, where you actually used the system of the university to try and create generators?

65. (From left to right) Cedric Price and Bernard Tschumi, c. 1990

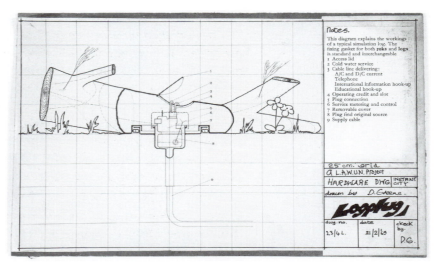

66. David Greene/Archigram, Logplug, 1967 (Credit: David Greene/Archigram Archives)

67. François Barré took on the cultural direction of the Parc and gave it its initial impetus

68. Serge Goldberg was the key governmental representative who supported the Parc and made it possible for it to be built

27. Cedric Price also entered the competition for the Parc de La Villette, proposing a combined architectonic and telecommunications network overlaid onto the site. Bernard Tschumi had the opportunity later on, once much of the La Villette scheme was in place, to invite Price to contribute a design for the Parc. Price's SERRE scheme for a greenhouse for roses is published in Vaisseau de Pierres 2: Parc de la Villette (Champ Vallon, 1987), pp 61–3.

Bernard Tschumi   I have realised one thing now – that you really set me up this morning!
You have placed me in a very psychoanalytic situation! Starting with
my father, then mentioning Alvin Boyarsky (who was very important to
me), and Peter, who has been a father in a way. Now, Nigel is more of a
brother, and he [Carlos] is probably an illegitimate son [Laughter]. All of
that's very important in regards to this strange English component that
Peter mentioned. Nothing in my background predisposed me to have any
connection with England. I knew continental Europe, I knew the States,
but I came to England only because of what was happening in architecture
around people like Cedric Price,[65] not because of English culture.
I actually wanted to work for Cedric and I had, in fact, invited him to the
ETH in Zurich when I was a student representative. The teachers said:
'No, you can't, because that's not architecture.' So you see why I liked
Cedric so much. And then I ended up teaching at the AA.[27]

Peter mentioned a word, 'eccentric'. It is the word for not being a
conformist, but also for not being an anti-conformist. Being 'eccentric' is
sort of doing one's own thing, testing the grounds, but quite often having
an extraordinary independence in terms of un-official ways of doing
things. That freedom of thinking in architecture is very rare. Most of the
time people work within canons. You know the phrase a 'canonic' building,
meaning one that is made within almost-religious rules? And then
suddenly, there he is [Bernard identifies David Greene in the audience]
– someone doing his own thing, which he called Rokplug or Logplug[66] –
and suddenly that is described as being part of the realm of architecture!
So for the French or Swiss student I was at the time that certainly made
you open your eyes.

As for the rigid framework of the grid and how to determine it: once the
notion of the points was established, making it operational was not that
difficult, for two reasons. The first is that you have a site, you have a
number of site constraints, and the reality principle takes over. In other
words, you know that you can't put something here (because you have the
water) or here (because you have the highway). You don't want to make
things too difficult for yourself, so you don't put three <u>folies</u> right over
the motorway. You need to find a certain density. You also have some sort
of programme. So, you arrive at the density in such a way that you are
combining a very abstract concept, but always a concept that has a grip
on reality, and you test it out very quickly. If it doesn't work in the first few
days – in your office or on your kitchen table or whatever – you throw it
away because it means that it is a no-good concept. I think that is what
happened with the standard grid.

The more interesting part was the unforeseen advantage of the point
grid. I remember the late evenings I was spending with one person –
not François Barré,[67] whom you alluded to earlier and who was the
remarkable head of programming for the client at La Villlette, but rather
someone called Serge Goldberg,[68] who was the head of construction. We
were literally spending time together like chess players over a chessboard
with full knowledge of the political pressures on the many people who
wanted to kill the Parc. Another party had come into power, and there
were people who wanted to replace the Parc with housing – there was

69. Tightrope walker traversing space between <u>folies</u>

28. McLean has vague recollections that
Tschumi secured him an honorary AA
Diploma (<u>not</u> a degree) in acknowledgement
of his contribution to the unit's activities.

29. St Martin's School of Art, London,
founded in 1854. McLean studied sculpture
there from 1963 to 1966, with classes taken
by a number of well-known artists of the
time including Sir Anthony Caro.

even a project for the Olympics – and we were scheming together by asking which folie should be built first and where. Should we build the ones at the centre first, or here at the sides, so as to at least have coherence, so that if the project were stopped we would at least have a mini-park? And then we went with a totally different strategy. We said, no, we are not going to start with the entrances – people will have to enter in any case, so we can build this one later. So we located some folies at specific distances apart so that we knew we would have to fill in the gaps later, and we consciously built them so that, at the beginning, there was no coherence. It really looked tragic! So much of the planning was strategic and very pragmatic; the concept itself may be highly abstract, but it had to have the ability to evolve little by little, in a pragmatic way.

Bruce McLean I am very interested in what you are supposed to have said about Cedric Price – that he didn't make architecture or he wasn't an architect. Did you say that?

Bernard Tschumi No, one of my teachers said that.

Bruce McLean But that is surely what interested you in him. But what interests me about what you've been doing is the fact that you had the kind of intelligence to actually associate yourself with artists, writers and other people, which I think has affected how you've proceeded. I am indebted to you of course for my degree[28] because you came and saw something I was doing, and I'm also as interested as you are in looking at things another way and having a concept of something. But the thing that I'm not interested in is art – and I suspect that you are not actually interested in architecture, actually. But what they seem to talk about in architecture school is architecture, and what they talk about in art school is art, so I would like to propose that we get together more. I can't believe that there is a situation here with so many architects actually supporting each other. I think it's quite spectacular, really. I can't imagine this in an art school at all! But, back to your grid situation – I think the grid is great! [Laughter] But what I find tricky about this morning is that we've gone along in a bloody line [Referring to the seating of the critics]. You did say [Much hand gesturing around the audience] it's all about the grid! What I think is really interesting about these pavilions or folies, that you haven't really discussed yet, is that they are like behaviour stations – aren't they? Do people actually participate in these? Is that what you wish to occur? I quite like them empty, I have to say.

Bernard Tschumi Is that you up there? [Points to a slide showing an acrobat on a tightrope**69**]

Bruce McLean In earlier times it might have been me! I think that is the longest 'pose pole' in the world actually [Laughter]. It is very good that you actually had, at an earlier moment in time, the intelligence to actually work across things. I think there is a real problem in schools of art and in architecture that philosophers aren't in there, writers aren't in there. I was fortunate to go to St Martins[29] where there were philosophers and writers teaching, but now it doesn't seem to be the case. I'm very pleased to be here to see this marvellous work, and we will get back to the grid too a little later on.

70. Bernard Tschumi in a still from the film <u>Sound Distance of a Good Man</u> by Robert Longo

71. David Salle, <u>High and Low</u>, 1994 (Credit: © David Salle/VAGA, New York/DACS)

72. Cindy Sherman, <u>Untitled Film Still #17</u>, 1978 (reprinted 1998)

30. Michael Graves (1934–), American architect and one of the New York Five (see p 42). His postmodern style is at its most playful and entertaining at the Swan and Dolphin Hotels, Disney, Florida and most sober at the iconic Portland Building, Portland, Oregon. Graves is also well known for his furniture and product designs.

31. Kate Linker, art critic and writer of books on art including <u>Love for Sale: The Words and Pictures of Barbara Kruger</u> (Harry N. Abrams Inc., 1990) and <u>Vito Acconci</u> (Rizzoli, 1994), among others.

Bernard Tschumi   Well, the issue of 'art and architecture' is actually rather painful, because why should those categories be so hard-edged? At the time when Bruce and I were playing with ideas and talking together, we referred to it as 'the sensibility'. The relationship between the two terms was extremely close. There were not too many differences between the way Bruce McLean was thinking here in London, and the way friends of mine like Robert Longo,[70] David Salle[71] or Cindy Sherman[72] were working in New York. But the funny thing is that you could produce work without caring whether it was called 'art' or 'architecture', as part of a common exploration.

About four years before La Villette, people started to come to the New York loft where I lived and worked to see my work. Some of them invited me to exhibit in art galleries. Then I was formally asked by two galleries at the same time. One was called Metro Pictures, the other the Max Protetch Gallery. I had only admiration for the artists showing at Metro Pictures (who included Cindy Sherman and Longo, among others) and less interest for the work of Michael Graves[30] and a few other architects at Max Protetch. By then I was very close to an art critic named Kate Linker,[31] and when I mentioned that I had been approached by Metro Pictures, she said: 'No way! You're not an artist, you're an architect!' Psychoanalysis, right? So I exhibited at the architects' gallery. The reason why I tell this story is that the social and professional pressures are such that, even if you want to fight against received ideas, you often end up caught up in them. If you always try to travel the road that accompanies freedom, then you are really stuck as an architect because your clients are banks, governments and other establishment people. So we are caught in that strange situation where we have to manoeuvre in order to give the appearance of respectability. Therefore, we call ourselves architects.

Nigel Coates   It is difficult to focus the La Villette design on the issue of movement because that can never be repeated. It is represented and frozen and in a sense conformed to all the freezing tendencies architecture has performed since time immemorial. But that means that the actual movement and the actual experiences which take place in the spaces you've created, is another step. How much do you think that you were able to anticipate what those occupations would be? Did you want to anticipate them, or did you want to cause the absolute opposite, where nothing was determined about how the spaces would be used? Of course the cubes are the clearest example of that point. Where the cubes, as I understand it, have certain prescribed functions – whether it is a kindergarten or a club – but then they translate choreography into three dimensions. They are not just flat, not just a wall – they have a kind of balletic, sculptural engagement. So when they were built, were you surprised or disappointed by the way people used them – were ordinary people able to live up to what you expected them to do?

Bernard Tschumi   YES! Before getting to people, I should touch on the issue of frozen movement. Maybe it goes back to the arts scene of the time, when a number of artists were interested in B-movies and had taken images and freeze-framed them, as one calls it. So sure, you could think that the movement that you have drawn on a piece of paper and eventually build

73. One of several opening days with President Mitterrand

74. The unprogrammed Parc

is a 'frozen' movement, and therefore on some level an authoritarian constraint. This is partly true, but not completely.

In the case of La Villette, it was done consciously. There were certain movements that were highly documented, like those involving accelerated movement. We knew that there were people who were in a hurry to get from A to B, and then there was a distended, elongated movement for people who wanted a more mysterious, romantic walk. But at certain moments the two intersect, and we thought of those moments as points of unpredictability because we couldn't know what was going to happen. So, in other words, we would design conditions that were very precise but that had totally unpredictable intersections. That was point number one. Point number two: the actual surfaces. The flat surfaces in between the points are totally free for people to do whatever they want. I know that whenever I explained the project, I tended to be relatively didactic about the points and the lines. But with the surfaces, I tended to obfuscate or hide the fact that here [Pointing to open spaces on the exploded axonometric, see p 19] a lot of random movements happen. Random movements go along with random activities.

Let me give you three examples of things that were not 'expected'. The first (which is, in a sense, emotional) happened when things were sufficiently built to open up a little chunk of the Parc. I go there, and there is still nobody there because the Parc has not yet been opened officially by President Mitterrand,[73] and I walk around. Nobody there – just thousands of birds that have taken the place over, making an unbelievable racket. I'm sure you know, or will find out, that when one of your buildings gets to a certain stage, it's a very emotional reaction when you see it. I was absolutely amazed. And then I saw people taking over the place. They seemed to be coming out of nowhere, and the last people I wanted to see were the ones playing boules. They had found a flat place made out of thin gravel that was perfect for them. Not a programme we had in mind, right? The second group of people who came were also not planned because the client didn't want them: the football players, particularly the ones wearing cleats. They began taking over some of the triangle areas. The third group whom we'd never thought about were the musicians. In the meandering promenade, you have people constantly playing drums, in any season: no trumpets, no guitars, just drums. Also not planned, right? Then, of course, you have the lovers, the families, the open-air cinema, etc. The Parc was sufficiently unprogrammed for all of this to happen, quite spontaneously.[74]

It was important that you had buildings that you didn't know what they were for – some had functions, but they also changed function many times. The point was that what we designed was a support, a sort of anchor for people's imaginations. One was a painting and sculpture workshop for little kids who built cardboard folies for themselves. They were always asked to do the exercise 'Design the next one', and they made some wonderful things. I was very pleased; I'm still very pleased (and this is unusual) to go to the Parc. So, yes, a lot of things happened and still happen there that I never expected, including things that are highly illegal in France and England. Why not?

75. Piano + Rogers, Pompidou Centre, Paris, 1977

32. Manfredo Tafuri (1935–94), Italian architect, Marxist architectural historian and architectural theorist. Publications include <u>Theories and History of Architecture</u> (Granada, 1980) and <u>Architecture and Utopia: Design and Capitalist Development</u> (MIT Press, 1976).

33. The Guggenheim Museum in Bilbao (Frank Gehry, 1997) came to exemplify a condition of revitalising cities through tourism at the turn of this century. Since Bilbao no longer thrived as the centre of Spain's steel industry and as a busy port, the city has reinvented itself as a major cultural port by working with the Solomon R. Guggenheim Foundation to commission an internationally renowned 'star' architect to build a major public building as a catalyst for further new development.

Paul Finch   At the design stage, if you didn't envisage football or <u>boules</u> – perhaps because you didn't like the idea of an unconventional place being used in conventional ways – did you have any idea for what those spaces might be used for? Were there alternatives that didn't occur?

Bernard Tschumi   Well, my idea included a running track and similar things. But I didn't want to do artificial nature. It wasn't going to be Hyde Park, so we constructed the green spaces or fields absolutely flat, which infuriated the landscape architects. If you want a field that is really flat, you have to drain it – you know, it rains in France, too – and there is only one proper technology. It's the technology of the football field. So that is what the green spaces were, but hidden! But of course, the football players noticed.

Murray Fraser   That takes me on to another question I wanted to ask. I was going to mention Manfredo Tafuri[32] and ask whether there was a subversive political intent in this project at all. Manfredo Tafuri had used many of the theories you mentioned – from people like Foucault, Derrida, etc – to demolish the myths of modernism, to argue that there was no architecture possible under capitalism, that there were no hopes in design. And so the question is whether you and architects like Koolhaas were trying to use those same theorists to argue that there were chances of creating counter-values? You wrote later, I believe, of using judo tactics against the forces of power – the people who have control of society. So, I want to know, was this a conscious strategy in the project? And, is there then perhaps a critical reading of this project, in the sense of a tokenism by the French state to allow avant-garde practices loose – because it's only an abattoir in a slightly remote part of Paris – and then keep the buildings of power in the centre of the city, and give those projects to established architects who will design conventional buildings?

Bernard Tschumi   I am going to give you a very untheoretical answer. First of all, I haven't had a chat about this with Rem, but I don't think Manfredo Tafuri (when he was alive) ever went to see any of our buildings. The French government – or any government today, including in Greece or South Korea – is increasingly interested, when it decides to build this type of project, in making a place that, in a sense, becomes a symbol for something else, a sort of identity of something. I would date this syndrome to before Bilbao,[33] probably starting with the Pompidou Centre,**75** because the Sydney Opera House was something else altogether. Nobody expected the extraordinary success of the Pompidou Centre. The successes were visual, cultural and technological. Nobody had ever seen anything like that – they used to call it the 'oil refinery'. And its ideas remain current today.

Problematic? Well, it was a place that was supposed to offer something for everybody and to become a sort of generator of activities. For me, that model was still more or less in the background when I did La Villette. It was certainly in the minds of the people who wrote the programme for La Villette from the client's point of view. Technological? That was particular to France. In the early 1970s, France was really backward in terms of architecture and architectural engineering, and there is a story that one of the real reasons Piano + Rogers won the Pompidou competition was because the French government and its high civil

76. George Trakas, <u>Transfer Station</u>, 1978. Installation, Art Gallery of Ontario, 13 May–9 July 1978. Part of an exhibition called <u>Structures for Behaviour</u>

77. Snow-covered Parc de la Villette

34. Reference to 'Arupism', a term coined by Luigi Prestinenza Puglisi in Supercrit #3: The Pompidou Centre, 22 April 2005.

35. A fundamental characteristic of Postmodernist style and philosophy is the concept of the arrangement of fragmentary information – the mixing of reality (historical reference) with hyper reality (fluid subjectivity and simulation) – and therefore the relationship between author/designer and reader/viewer.

servants wanted Ove Arup to come and work in France.[34] It was as if no building could generate both technological and cultural images. Today, everybody is trying to re-enact the Bilbao effect. So it is no longer about subversion, but rather something that has more to do with tourism, like any product branding or logo design. To return to your Tafuri example, I think here he would have liked to be left out of it – architecture as brand.

Paul Finch   I want to come back to Bruce McLean briefly, to get out of this linear sequence. It's also because I want to ask you a question. Going back to something that was said about people and the way they use this space – is this the equivalent of the old tag about the Postmodern condition where the viewer completes the picture,[35] for La Villette and for parks generally? The notion of what goes on in them, the people who come to them and how they behave, is much more integral to both the underlying programme of the project and to its outcome than is ever the case in conventional architecture. So is this why perhaps one can see La Villette, whatever the technology being exploited, as an artwork rather than a piece of architecture?

Bruce McLean   Yes, I think it is a piece of artwork. I am actually fascinated by the fact that you actually managed to do it. You had a wonderful concept that you actually managed to do. I'd never seen any photographs of anybody in it … until today. I thought that was very good because parks in the end are for nobody. You can't do this, you can't do that – a big 'Park of NO' is something I'd like to work on. To have enormous amounts of space to do absolutely nothing in, that nobody would actually go to – do you know what I mean? Because there is so much stuff around it, we need to put an empty space. I am going to go and look at La Villette in a couple of weeks time and wander around it and behave in it. I am quite interested in the work of George Trakas**76** who made behaviour stations. Remember him? I thought they were quite interesting spaces that you can go and stand on or lie down or leave.

I feel it's quite inspirational, but actually if I had done this project I'd be more concerned about the behaviour of the people in the space, how they would behave. Not controlling their behaviour, but making them behave in other ways, you know [Pointing to a slide of a folie], that could be the Department of Redundant Gestures, just like that [Makes a redundant gesture with his arm], for example … did you see that?

Bernard Tschumi   Yes. I don't want to make people behave a certain way, because that is none of my business; I want to give them the opportunity to behave the way they want to, right? If you go to La Villette, let's say on 1 February, when it has just snowed and the Parc is entirely deserted, the snow looks perfect and you hear nothing. It is really beautiful.**77** I hate green, which is why I like the Parc at that time of year so much. So that is an unusual situation of having a place that changes appearances. But something that I try to do in every project – literally every one – is to develop conditions of public space or public interaction. You know, even in the Lausanne 'Bridge-City' project, the important thing was lifting up a part of the project so as to have large public spaces that

78. Buttes Chaumont Park was commissioned by Emperor Napoleon III and built on the site of a former limestone quarry, mined for the construction of buildings in Paris and the USA. The park was designed by Baron Haussmann with engineer Jean-Charles Alphand, and opened in 1867 as part of the Universal Exhibition

79. François Mitterrand (1916–96), President of France 1981–95, elected representative of the Socialist Party, standing in front of La Géode at the Parc de la Villette (Credit: © Thierry Orban/Corbis Sygma)

80. The gardens of the Palace of Versailles as laid out in the 17th Century

81. Oscar Niemeyer, the Cathedral of Brasilia (under construction), completed 1970

were unprogrammed, where people could do whatever they wanted, including art installations and so on. The public realm today is increasingly privatised. Entire pieces of the city are built by private capital, and public art is sponsored. Much of the objective of the work, if one wants to be seriously sociological (which I don't think we really should), is about that urban public space and public interaction in the city. That will be my only political statement today.

Paul Finch   But in a very different way to Bilbao.

Peter Cook   In the late 1980s, I did actually take a very special person to your park, and not as a direct result of the red pavilion concerned, but the lady later consented to marry me and it was a very important part of a sequence of events. So I have been one of your consumers!

I can remember though, on another occasion before that, when you took me to eat around the corner from La Villette at another park; a funny, spooky old park with grottos and a lake that is only half a mile away.**78** It doesn't use red metal; it uses old bits of concrete got up to look like Bluebeard's Castle and some funny island, some old clay pit, or something. And I'm wondering, to what extent was that over your shoulder (probably as a hate object), all the things that that park does, or all the things that your park does not do, sitting just around the corner. The anti-body. The 'other' park in that district of Paris. The other thing that I wouldn't mind dragging in briefly is that I seem to remember, as with the Piano + Rogers office before you, there were very few French people working in your office, probably actually, none. They [Piano + Rogers] had virtually none either, and I wondered if you wanted to be regarded as a French architect? I don't know what passport you carry, but you never wanted to be seen as one, and you've said that on many occasions I think.

Bernard Tschumi   No, I'm not a French architect. I'm not a Swiss architect. I'm not an American architect. I am simply an architect. Two things: first, I now have very good French people working in my office, but at the beginning of the project, that certainly was not the case.

Second, let me tell you a story about the Buttes Chaumont Park, which you mentioned, and what you called 'the offset'. When we won the competition, I didn't yet have an office. I had a small apartment in Paris, so we set up an office with three people in the living room, just for the first month or two. I had to present the project to the French president, François Mitterrand.**79** We prepared an enormous board, and I simply put together four drawings on it. The first was of Versailles,**80** the grand park in the royal French tradition – the axis, the symmetries, the rows of planting. The second showed the Buttes Chaumont – the Romantic park, built in the 19th century, the sort where you would see Byron and that sort of figure, along with fake grottos made out of crumbling concrete. Then the third drawing was of Brasilia**81** under construction, and I said – here I was being mean – that it was the park of the 20th century. And then, the last one, number four, was an image of La Villette, the park of the 21st century. I showed the board to President Mitterrand, and

82. Bernard Tschumi Architects, West Diaoyutai Tower, Beijing, China.
First Prize, 2004 competition. 59,000 square metre luxury hotel and apartment building

36. Diploma 10 is an undergraduate unit at the Architectural Association run by Carlos Villanueva Brandt since 1986.

he looks at all the images like that [Poses studiously] and stays silent in front of the La Villette drawing. Then he goes back to the first two and says, well, they were pretty good, after all! I have to say he was extremely supportive later on. But in answer to your question, I was very aware of those things … but I'm always glad to hear more of the private stories.

Paul Finch   I want to ask a question of Carlos about when you are talking to students and citing La Villette as an example. Are there any <u>health</u> warnings about what's been learnt from this project in terms of the approach, the programme or indeed the outcome?

Carlos Villanueva Brandt   Yes, lots of warnings and also a question to you, Bernard, too, which is: is there life after La Villette? In a sense – and I think one of the things that is very interesting in terms of, let's say, the research that is being done at the moment in Diploma 10 at the AA[36] – is whether it would be possible on a much larger scale, not 120 metres, but a <u>much larger</u> scale, to create an urban strategy which was generated by three different sets of people? So that some people were doing the points, some people doing lines and some people doing surfaces. How would you achieve that politically? How would you work with it and what kind of environment would you need? So the important thing to point out to students would be that La Villette was 'contained'.

You've answered many of the issues in relation to other questions, but if you were to do this scheme as a bigger thing, i.e. where the political forces, the economic forces became even more complex so that they were no longer within your remit, the remit of one person, then how do you see the future possibilities of that? Do you think that La Villette can become an urban strategy? And secondly, some thoughts: whilst looking at your office's website, it was interesting to see the work in the Far East – I tell the students – a bit more on the non-warning side – that I feel that they should look at your work because you do deal with culture which I think is important because a lot of architecture at the moment doesn't look at culture in any way. But what about China? What happens there? You designed a tower,[82] which is not directly related but can one actually begin to set out an urban strategy like this, such as La Villette, in so alien a culture, or in one which is moving so fast that it becomes quite difficult to even lay things out?

Bernard Tschumi   You are asking many questions. The general one that I will answer first is that, in terms of strategies, there are so many different ones. One shouldn't take La Villette literally, try to change its scale, and use it elsewhere. But – and here I'll keep the word that is now being debated, 'strategy' – I'm all in favour of looking at ways to generate urban life, or to find ways in which architecture can be something that <u>does</u> things instead of <u>looking like</u> things. I always say that I'm not interested in what something looks like; I'm interested in what it does. The other point, amusingly enough, and the more personal one, which relates to the first part of your question: sure, it changes your life, in a way. I have tried, in terms of our work in the office, to keep a distance from La Villette. When we published the first project book about the office, I did not include

83. Questions from the audience

37. The Event-Cities series is published by MIT Press. The first volume was published in 1994. Event-Cities 2, published in 2000, includes the Parc de la Villette on pp 44–223.
38. See Further reading.

La Villette.[37] We have never done a big book on La Villette, though we might one day.[38] This was done on purpose: because of the scale of the project, it would swallow up everything else; after all, we worked on it for 15 years, right? So the issue – and now I am back to your other point about 'strategies' – is that I really believe that architecture is made out of a number of concepts and ideas that can have an incredible effect on both the history or nature of the discipline, but also on the everyday life of people. If you go back to the three parks in Paris that have been built, people talked about them as the parks of the future, the present, and the past. People called La Villette the 'park of the future,' which is nice. But what's interesting is that it is the one where the activities are unpredictable – that it is the only one that has had a social impact.

Paul Finch   Can I ask if there are any persons in the audience with a question? I'll take a couple and then come back to Bernard for a response.

Unidentified student 1[83]   I'm particularly interested in how you managed to transform an abstract project like The Manhattan Transcripts into a reality at La Villette, and I want to ask you this: you say The Manhattan Transcripts derived from attempting to create your own vocabulary in architecture but that is 25 years old now. So if you had to do a student project for this time next week, say for another crit in a week's time, and you had to redefine today's rules, how would you go about it and what would you do differently in relation to The Manhattan Transcripts?

Unidentified student 2   You mention about building this scheme as something that was built from your text, and you mention the words 'practicing theory' and 'theoretical practice'. So I am going to pick up on the ideas of practicing theory. Something that you mention as an intention would be event and the cinematic. How would you assess this project based on the scale of elements, say if the folies would be normal huts or the lines would be just normal promenades or the scale of the Parc in relation to the city? But, what is its success compared to Hyde Park in London, or maybe compared to Downsview in Toronto which is the inverse? How does practising theory become useful to you? Is it merely a tool for formal interpretation of the subjective judgement?

Paul Finch   Nice simple questions, then!

Bernard Tschumi   To the first question: if I had to do another project in one week and present it here, forget it! What I found out is that it's very quick to come to a form; it's very slow to arrive at a concept. So things just don't happen in a week. In the case of The Manhattan Transcripts, perhaps the major lesson that I learned from it, and that still occasionally comes back in my work today, is the notion of independent and autonomous systems that work without any reference to one another and are superimposed on one other. Also, it was very useful to have explored a specific series of devices in The Manhattan Transcripts. I was not bound by the usual architectural clichés of architectural representation because I was inventing the rules as I went along. Maybe that was the closest I got to behaving like an artist.

The question about practicing theory and theory preceding practice or practice preceding theory – well, I have always hated the idea of a clear

39. One previous explanation appears in an image caption in Event-Cities 2: 'Because red is not a colour'. Event-Cities 2 (MIT Press, 2000), p 167.

'outcome' or cause-and-effect relationship. In the 1980s and 1990s, especially in America, a lot of people were saying that you had to have a theory on which to base your design. But one of the great things about architecture, and about projects in general, is that they force you to think along, or through, some sort of an object, or what we would call a 'project'. We 'project' ourselves toward it and organise our thoughts together with the project. I mentioned that at a certain moment a good project will begin to work for you: it will help you think. So you have to be a very good editor. Peter, in the context of running the Diploma Year at the AA you spoke about the importance of editing, deciding what goes in and what doesn't. One of the greatest gifts you can have is discipline. It often happens that you have the theoretical concept, implement it, and then develop it practically, but it also happens that the practical development can take you to another theoretical concept. You had better recognise it. Sometimes you don't immediately recognise it – it maybe takes a year to 'get' that theoretical concept. But it is absolutely crucial as an architect to be able to be objective, to stand back from the work and have an overview.

Bruce McLean   Can I ask a quick question? It's a straightforward question. You are obviously invited to do things now, but prior to La Villette you entered a competition, which you won. Do you dream still – of things you'd like to do? Do you have another dream about Paris or Shanghai and make doodles and notes and then present that <u>without</u> being invited?

Bernard Tschumi   I don't ask myself this question, so maybe you are right to ask it. Yes, I do, but, funnily enough, I don't do doodles.

Bruce McLean   But do you <u>invent</u> the project?

Bernard Tschumi   A good question, which goes back to a conversation that Nigel Coates and I had a long time ago about the 'second programme'. The first programme is the one given to you by the client, and then you have to reformulate the programme into something that you invent, which interests you.

Paul Finch   I'll take one more question from the audience and then we will run along the line (but in reverse order!) just to get a final comment about what you think La Villette means to you, to architecture, to Paris, to ideas.

Unidentified student 3   Can I just ask why red?

Bernard Tschumi   After so many years, that is still the only question I never answer. [Laughter and applause][39]

Carlos Villanueva Brandt   I think that because of your explanation, it has probably been a very good crit. You might have got a bit more than C– or C+. I think that the project is extremely influential, and that is what is interesting about the work. I'm not saying you're not a nice guy, it's just that the strength of La Villette, in my opinion, is that it's the project itself that one tends to quote, it makes people think. One really admires it as a project.

**84. 'The whole Parc is a folly'
(Nigel Coates)**

**85. Bernard Tschumi shows Queen Elizabeth II plans for the Parc
prior to its completion**

40. Leopold Bloom, the main protagonist in James Joyce's Ulysses (Silvia Beach, 1922).

41. Marcel Proust, Swann's Way (1913), the first volume of the seven-part masterpiece Remembrance of Things Past. Neither Joyce's nor Proust's works are constructed as linear narratives, but rather as collections of memories recalled in a stream-of-consciousness.

42. The Cultural Revolution c. 1965–9. A political campaign led by Chinese Communist Party Chairman Mao Zedong to renew the spirit of the Chinese revolution; to suppress, by violence, the emergence of a privileged or bourgeois class, and destroy 'old ways of thinking'.

Peter Cook   The great thing about the fact that you won the competition is that it showed the profession that somebody who can teach and draw and write, can build, and that was tremendously inspirational – and that you did it rather well was also a help. That was the big breakthrough.

Murray Fraser   I think for me what has come out today is the complexity of this project. A lot of the questions touched on all these different aspects. But, if there is a tie between the clear concepts that you like to put forward for the project and the ideas of the experience of space – the two things you try to work together – then, for me, the clear concept seems to win, both in the way it is presented and in the way you discuss it. One is always struck when you go to La Villette, that in all the richness of being there, the things which you really experience are those two enormous functional axes that draw people into the Parc. I think in this sort of dialectic that it is that side which probably always comes out ahead.

Nigel Coates   I like the project more than I've ever liked it before, so that's good! I now love it! [Laughter]. I thought it was intriguing when you said that there are all sorts of things going on in these trees here that you didn't know about, and then it occurred to me that the whole Parc is a folly.**84** In a curious way it returns to Versailles, which was the implementation of power; the straightening out of the Italian garden, making it something of the State. And, although you showed all those different images to Mitterrand, I wonder if there is more of a loop between them than I had realised before.**85**

Bernard Tschumi   I don't want to respond to all of you; I just want to thank all of you, not only for this morning but, in the case of the front row, for what they have given me personally over the years. There is no doubt that La Villette would not have been possible without all of you. Also, thanks to the audience because you are also part of the conversation.

Paul Finch   To finally conclude, well, the editor has to have the last word doesn't he?

I think we went on a very interesting journey because there is a criticism, in Britain certainly, that we are a literary and not visual nation, and yet what we've heard this morning is actually that certain informing ideas about this project come from James Joyce in Covent Garden. Bloom[40] – what an inspiration for a park! We end up with a latter-day Proust, a sort of Swann's Way[41] across a historical and creative landscape in that most radical and yet conservative of cities, Paris.

France was the first European country to create a conservation and heritage body to protect the past. It did that right after the Revolution, when it suddenly realised that the enthusiasm for demolishing everything aristocratic might result in some rather beautiful and valuable things vanishing from the face of the earth. So the French did what Mao, of course, never did – the latter choosing to destroy what was wonderful rather than save it.[42] The French attitude to the past is both deeply respectful and deeply suspicious, and I find an interesting parallel in this project when I begin to think it wasn't actually about deconstructing anything; it was about destabilising something – which is not quite the

86. Competition for the Bibliothèque Nationale, Paris (1988) – model of the entry by Futuresystems. Dominique Perrault won the competition and his completed scheme was opened in 1996

87. The Thames Gateway, north Kent coast, UK (Credit: Will McLean)

43. Nigel Whiteley, <u>Reyner Banham: Historian of the Immediate Future</u> (MIT Press, 2002).

44. Paul Finch's own re-working of R. Buckminster Fuller's neologisms: 'Humanity has the option to become successful on our planet if we reorient world production away from weaponry – from killingry to livingry. Can we convince humanity in time?'

same thing. Was it Cedric's wonderful phrase – or perhaps it was Reyner Banham's – about architects writing the history of the immediate future,[43] and in doing competition entries and then winning them, of course that is what they do.

The theme of destabilisation instead of deconstruction would explain the parallels of having an apparently deconstructed piece of city and a completely new piece of city. Yet, as we've heard, the grid underlying it is entirely rational because, as Bernard correctly concluded, the French were going to have a grid. If not, it wasn't made rational and there might be a bit of trouble! How prescient that was, because we then had I.M. Pei's Louvre Pyramid, and the Bibliothèque Nationale, which Futuresystems probably should have won,[86] but with I.M. Pei advising Mitterrand, of course they preferred the imposing orthogonal grid in the scheme [built] by Dominique Perrault.

On the structural side, what Peter Rice might have said is what you've played with is not the idea of destabilised structures but with eccentric structures. I mean that in the engineering sense, not in the English sense of eccentric, though there is an element of that which I think infuses the whole project. This is a folly writ large.

The question about what happens if you take this analysis and start running it out at a hyper-scale across chunks of city – or to take a more local example, run it out across the Thames Gateway[87] – a landscape project which is pretending to be a housing solution – who knows where that might lead! I don't think that sort of imaginative leap is on the mind of the present UK administration, which I think is a great pity.

What we have heard this morning is a clarity of presentation and expression, which is itself a mark of the clarity of thinking which went into a project where the diagram – a neglected subject in architecture – was important. It was not a project that derived from messing around with visualisations on a computer screen, where every time you punch a button you complete a line. The beautiful analytical drawings of the nature of that grid are a great encouragement to remind students and practicing designers about that moment between 'project-ry' and 'design-ry':[44] the concept, the analysis, the crystallising moment when the project starts to work for you. That is the moment where you can draw it out, because that's the moment when it's moving rather than being in a sort of whirling cosmos.

Thank you all very much.

Helen Castle watched Parc de la Villette receive the Supercrit treatment

Tschumi faces the family

The Supercrit is now establishing itself as a highlight of the academic London year, creating a unique buzz with a departure from the manner in which architecture is usually discussed.

Organised by the Research Centre for Experimental Practice at the University of Westminster, it has transformed "the crit" into a masterclass format with the potential mischief, as regular chair Paul Finch observed, of "a whole load of impertinent questions".

Following Richard Rogers' presentation of the Pompidou Centre last April, Bernard Tschumi's Parc de la Villette in north-east Paris was the subject of last week's event. Tschumi won the project by competition in 1982, transforming the former meat market and slaughterhouse into Paris's largest park, populated with bright red structures for a variety of uses.

Tschumi embraced the Supercrit experience with all the diligence of a final-year student, arriving half an hour early and rearranging drawings for the jury's and audience's scrutiny at the front of the room. He was dressed for the occasion in dark trousers, white shirt and a fire-engine red scarf. The red may match his constructivist follies at la Villette, but it was a predilection — as we found out from Peter Cook — that was already established in his Architectural Association days with his red pullovers.

Standing with his back to the window, Tschumi was faced with a jury that was dominated by

Tschumi (above) gave a stunning presentation on Parc de la Villette (right).

what he jested were his "AA family": Peter Cook "father"; Nigel Coates, "brother", and Carlos Villaneuva Brandt

"illegitimate son". Artist Bruce McLean and architectural historian Murray Fraser had also been thrown in for some semblance of balance. Such a regrouping always runs the risk of backslapping and out and out cosiness, but Cook, Coates and Villaneuva Brandt not only represent different generations at the AA, but very different preoccupations.

Tschumi's presentation was a tour de force. It is very rare to see a student audience totally enwrapped, the nonchalance knocked out of them by a single speaker. The experience was one of reading a virtuoso novelist when the possibility of ever writing like that yourself is moved even further away from you. Cook praised Tschumi for his unswerving "clarity" and it

was indeed the lucidity with which Tschumi spoke that was really stunning. Whereas at supercrit#3 Rogers met criticisms of the Pompidou Centre with a characteristic urbaneness and resigned humility, Tschumi was totally in the driving seat.

He opened with some anecdotes about his experiences of crits, before honing into the context of the AA in the late seventies and early eighties that led to Villette. He did away with the deconstructivist label by describing his engagement with Derrida's ideas as having the same currency as others at the time, whether it was Foucault or contemporary artists.

But it was his description of the "strategy" of the project that was bewitching and revealed his greatest strengths as an architect

Cook's reference to Tschumi's father was evidently something he was not comfortable with

and tactician. He showed the diagrams he had drawn up of conventional grids before deciding upon the point grid, which had the flexibility of "creating points of intensification that could be overlaid by vectors of movement"; a structure that could accommodate the sort of instability Tschumi craved, while also satisfying the French bureaucratic desire for a rational grid.

This understanding of tightness and looseness is intriguing. Cook traced it back to his education at ETH Zurich and Tschumi's beaux arts architect father. Cook's reference to his father was evidently something that Tschumi was not comfortable with and only "Cookie" could get away with.

It did, however, leave one with the impression that Tschumi's restrictive and rigorous education was as necessary to him as the inspired eccentricity of the AA in the seventies; it being only possible to effectively break the rules once you have gained the necessary grammar.
● *Helen Castle is editor of Architectural Design.*

REVIEW

Kester Rattenbury   At lunch, after Supercrit #4, Peter Cook said, 'Of course, it wasn't a real crit.' Coming from one of the critics, that was a somewhat backhanded comment, but I did agree with him. To those of us from the University of Westminster, Supercrit #4 had felt just a little too cosy, too AA-centric. The student had got the upper hand. We, the organisers, should have been tougher.

But actually, some students are like that at crits. They walk all over the critics. Bernard Tschumi simply stepped into the room, took a quick look round, took all the drawings but the site plan down (a trick he describes seeing done in his first jury) and took over. He praised and lauded the panellists, in advance, claiming them as his family; as collaborators in this project, deserving the credit with him, implicating them in the story he was about to tell. Any carefully phrased, thoughtfully couched criticism just slid off him. Infuriating.

So returning to the text, I am surprised to find how enlightening, how condensed and how clear – as Peter Cook commented – Supercrit #4 was. And how far the arguments I might have wished debated were, indeed, set out by Tschumi himself.

Though this was not a crit set in the field of deconstruction, Tschumi mentioned Jacques Derrida (whom he invited to work on a bit of the Parc): 'We should get one thing straight here: the Parc was hardly inspired by his theories … Derrida was more of an ally' and:

> When I first asked Derrida to come to my office, he immediately asked me: 'Why are you interested in deconstruction? Because deconstruction is anti-form, anti-hierarchy and anti-structure.' My answer was: 'Precisely for those reasons!'

With another jury, this might have provided the meat for a heated debate. But with a panel four-fifths loaded with colleagues and collaborators the recipe came out differently. 'I can't believe that there is a situation here with so many architects actually supporting each other. I think it's quite spectacular really, I can't imagine this in an art school at all!' said Bruce McLean. Fair comment.

Instead, Supercrit #4 was best on introducing newcomers to its context – the general spirit of the times; the sense of people who deliberately crossed disciplines, stole new tactics from other fields, like Bruce McLean's 'pose bands' – a kind of emblem of the knowing 'gestures' of the age. A time when architecture was trying to slip out of its seemingly mundane responsibilities. As a young man, Tschumi was warned:

> Bernard, if you are in London, don't call yourself an architect; call yourself a designer. Architects have very bad press. Architects are always responsible for the little old lady who gets stuck on the 17th floor of her social housing tower block whenever the lift breaks down!'

The interesting people – or perhaps the more progressive ones – of the time made paintings, drawings, exhibitions, performances, taught in art and architecture schools, even dipped into philosophy – did anything but straight architecture.

Tschumi was one of the leading figures of this age, with his speculative work based on cinematographic storyboards and advertisements, his drawings inspired by dance notation or the sequences of a fireworks display to describe movement in space. His book, The Manhattan Transcripts, shows a sequence of 'advertisements for architecture' – B-movie posters – one of which claimed 'To really appreciate architecture, you may even need to commit a murder.' That dealt with the mythical little old lady.

So, no responsibilities beyond refining the quality of ideas – and plenty of room to play. 'I don't know if I was that happy about the idea of winning La Villette – I was already really comfortable doing my own thing, and suddenly I had to open a real office,' said Tschumi. But being a park, there was room to continue playing and thinking. The series of tactics he used – overlaying geometries, the imposition of a grid – both strict and open-ended; the meandering cinematic route, mapping, ideas of fragmentation, performance, and experience are clearly (if sometimes, hyperbolically) described here:

> One concept was the most important concept of all – the one that could articulate a definition of architecture. That idea came from a prior work, The Manhattan Transcripts, which is all about space, movement and event. The idea was that all the horizontal planes in the drawings could unfold in the Parc as spaces to be appropriated by future users; throughout them, there are points of intensity and points of actions, specific locations where things 'happen'. Finally, there are the movement vectors, which designate movement through and around the Parc. The basic concept for the Parc, then, was the superimposition of points of intensity or events, a set of movement vectors (some very rigid, some extremely flexible and distended), and a set of planes. There were no constraints for the planes and I wouldn't design what would happen on them; this was not a park that was trying to recreate nature, but rather a piece of the city.
>
> It was important that the three systems could be superimposed onto one another, while maintaining their internal logic. That was new. Throughout architectural history, I don't think there were many people (or, in fact, anyone) who had accepted that the logic of movement or the logic of space or activity – in other words, three autonomous, independent logics with nothing to do with one another – could be brought together as heterogeneous systems, rather than trying to coordinate, reconcile, or harmonise the different constraints of a building. The superimposition brought about extraordinary tension. The logic of each plane might be resolved internally, but the juxtaposition would result in something entirely different that took the action or event that occurred in space as an integral part of the architectural definition.

One of the unexpected tactics was how the new office worked practically, in getting this formally unprecedented project built – on a huge site, with complex committees, with entirely different and often conflicting agendas such as sports, disabled access and the dominant urban history of Paris.

> It's possible that the point-grid that I had used led everybody to think, 'Oh, we can do anything.' Anybody could read anything into it. But at the same time, it gave us, as the architects … incredible power to provide a common denominator for often-conflicting agendas among different political constituencies, users and local inhabitants. So when I chose the point-grid, it was really as a strategy rather than as a project.

The funniest and most direct description of this strategy was how the design worked as a 'chess game' played by the contractor and Tschumi to get the whole of the Parc built – planning out the construction programme for the folies – while political factors suggested that the funding would be cut while the work was in progress:

> We were scheming together by asking which folie should be built first and where. Should we build the ones at the centre first, or here at the sides, so as to at least have a mini-park? And then we went with a totally different strategy. We said, no, we are not going to start with the entrances – people will have to enter in any case, so we can build this one later. So we located some of the folies at specific distances apart so that we knew we would have to fill in the gaps later, and we consciously built them so that, at the beginning, there was no coherence. It really looked tragic! So much of the planning was strategic and very pragmatic; the concept itself may be highly abstract, but it had to have the ability to evoke little by little, in a pragmatic way.

So – and rather like the Pompidou Centre (which Tschumi cited as a model) – the Parc de la Villette's surprise tactics ran it through a procurement system designed to produce quite different things, without touching the sides.

As a crit, this event delivered the raw ingredients, rather than the cooked meal, of a debate which is absolutely a central area for Tschumi's work: the difference between the drawn project – complex, multi-layered and open-ended, but inevitably formal, mannered, controlled – and the built experience – something Tschumi consciously aims at designing but knows he cannot possibly control – and how these realms interact.

Tschumi himself laid this out: 'It was a definition of architecture which was not necessarily about facades, about proportions, about harmony, as architects used to say, but about space, movement and event. A way of saying that architecture is both a space, and about what happens in that space.' Although Supercrit #4 described beautifully how this works, it left tantalisingly open the live question as to how it has played out in Tschumi's ongoing career as a major international architect.

To some extent, all the critics made forays that might have led into this area. Murray Fraser made two bold attempts: once, contrasting this park with his more recent competition design for Downsview in Toronto: Tschumi's neat answer was that Downsview was seen as a polemical opposite of La Villette; another question was about the political and social implications of the Parc, which Tschumi then compared with the Pompidou (whose political implications are more robustly discussed in Supercrit #3).

Any criticisms from those ever-ardent, expressive informal-formalists Nigel Coates and Peter Cook may have had of this project — or more likely, of Tschumi's later works — remained muted. They came closest to the surface in Cook's veiled allusions to Tschumi's recent project in Korea, to his father's architecture, and when Cook said:

> The point about being attracted to Derrida because of anti-form and anti-structure to me is a paradox. What Bernard has actually done in his architecture is to redefine form and it serves me to be highly concerned about structure.

While Coates, pulling at the ambiguity of tension and looseness in the drawings, also had the end of a line, which could end up somewhere central in this argument.

Bruce McLean was really the star critic and his point 'I suspect that you are not actually interested in architecture, actually' was enlightening here, and would be even more interesting to discuss in relation to Tschumi's current work: the Athens Museum. With its views of the Acropolis itself and its space designed for the Elgin Marbles (still in London), there's a powerful discussion to be had about staging events through architecture.

Tschumi's Athens building has been grossly underrated. It is a brilliant cinematic staging of experience, framing and sequencing your visit by direct juxtaposition with its spectacular site, its astonishing artefacts and — usually the bane of all museums — the crowds of other visitors, which here only manage to make the building look better. The museum is so successful at doing this that you do not notice it at all and its wry chic echoes of the temporary structures protecting the permanent working site of the Acropolis have been ignored or sneered at. It is a brilliant building but it is principally cinematic or experiential not formal, and its critics have failed to do it justice.

But the issue of Tschumi's later work — which many of his older friends are supposed to find boring, but which he strongly asserts is as good as ever but never given proper critical consideration (possibly because it is less formally expressive) — never surfaced nor Tschumi's chance to explain how he tries to design real events not formal analogies of them. A good smooth crit is not always the most helpful one.

But — just as the drawings of La Villette offered a compacted version from which one can unpack what the real project might be like — Supercrit #4 contained a kind of building set from which one can generate one's own detailed and extensive debate. Tschumi said:

> It is constantly unstable. There are all sorts of different publics, different users, at all different times of the day or night. It is a constantly changing environment, no matter what the weather.

And it is notable that on the one hand the design is described in terms of experiments, systems, forms and tactics, and (Tschumi would I am sure be pleased) as though the forms were incidental, but on the other hand that everyone describes the actual Parc purely in terms of experience.

Tschumi's own description of his first visit was particularly beautiful:

> I go there, and there is still nobody there because the Parc has not yet been opened by President Mitterrand, and I walk around. Nobody there – just thousands of birds that have taken the place over, making an unbelievable racket. I'm sure you know, or will find out, that when one of your buildings gets to a certain stage, it's a very emotional reaction when you see it. I was absolutely amazed. And then I saw people taking over the place. They seemed to be coming out of nowhere, and the last people I wanted to see were the ones playing boules. They had found a flat place made out of thin gravel that was perfect for them. Not a programme we had in mind, right? The second group of people who came were also not planned because the client didn't want them: the football players, particularly the ones wearing cleats. They began taking over some of the triangle areas.
>
> … I didn't want to do artificial nature. It wasn't going to be Hyde Park, so we constructed the green spaces or fields absolutely flat, which infuriated the landscape architects. If you want a field that is really flat, you have to drain it – you know, it rains in France too – and there is only one proper technology. It's the technology of the football field. So that is what the green spaces were, but hidden! But of course, the football players noticed.

Those football players made a critique – which no one else picked up – of Tschumi's interesting claims about parks and their formal and unpredictable qualities. Tschumi had, brilliantly, shown Mitterrand a panel with pictures of four parks:

> Versailles, the grand park in the royal French tradition – the axis, the symmetries, the rows of planting. The second showed the Buttes Chaumont – the Romantic park, built in the 19th century, the sort where you would see Byron and that sort of figure, along with fake grottos made out of crumbling concrete. Then the third drawing was of Brasilia under construction, and I said – here I was being mean – that it was the park of the 20th century. And then, the last one, number four, was an image of La Villette, the park of the 21st century … Mitterrand … goes back to the first two and says, well, they were pretty good, after all!

Mitterrand had a point. Tschumi's claim was that:

> If you go back to the three parks in Paris … what's interesting is that
> [La Villette] is the one where the activities are unpredictable – that it is
> the only one that has had a social impact.

It is unfortunate that none of the critics tackled this one. The football
players rumbled the project for what it (also) was – a park, in the tradition
of other parks, like Versailles, with its massive polemical statement about
man ordering nature for his own benefit, and with the king in the centre of
the universe. At La Villette similar tactics are applied ('actually, I don't like
nature very much') but with an opposite polemic: an open grid, accessible
to all; and deliberately layered up with alternative readings so that
everyone is at their own centre; and no one at anyone else's.

Perversely (as Tschumi suggested) landscape architecture is a great place
for architects to test the physical manifestation of pure ideas, because
its programme is so accommodating. You can theorise it without really
bothering anyone very much – from Versailles right across to Coney Island
– a proto-theme park which, according to Rem Koolhaas in Delirious
New York, can be retro-actively read as a rehearsal for the great anti-high-
architectural project of fantasy and congestion which was to be New York.
Parks can be raised to highest theory, or just enjoyed – that is what this
project is for.

> I'm really interested in these things because they are not about form, or
> about what architecture looks like, but about what it does. So in this
> respect, I think that, for me, every time, the design concept will come
> before the form.

Parc de la Villette was on the cusp of an ambiguous area between the
formal and the anti-formal – that same dilemma that Tschumi, Derrida and
Cook have pointed out: the strict but ruptured grid; the strong sculptural
presence, which can never be collected in a single photo or a single
visit. It is significant that it is impossible to photograph the 'whole thing',
challenging the very notion of what the 'whole thing' is. Tschumi's own
photos always show events rather than fictional 'definitive views' or key
shots beloved of traditional architectural photography. It is a deliberate
multiplicity – overlaying of ways of experiencing reading or seeing the
space by unknown people with unknown experiences of it. It is both
formal and anti-formal: as far as Tschumi is concerned, that is the whole
point.

But an awful lot of architects are – unsurprisingly – first and foremost
formalists. Not all, though. Tschumi set his stall out beautifully, and I am
personally disappointed this argument was not opened up more – either
by less polite critics or by those missing audience questions which were
sadly barely invited; variable in content and quality as questions are, they
do sometimes reveal the unexpected.

If the main aim of this review is to try to state that La Villette – by laying tactic on tactic and meaning on meaning – is absolutely crystallised in its drawn form, and absolutely uncapturable and subjective in its built form, it would suggest that architectural experience may occur in stages. It cannot be controlled, and the physical, photographable parts are a kind of theatrical prop, the stage scenery and machinery in this performance. As such a model, it has been a multi-layered and open-ended testing ground for much that was to come. And, for me, Tschumi's non-formal, programmatic, visual creations are the most underrated; as Samantha Hardingham says, they are – like Cedric Price's work – designed to liberate rather than confine.

This is the project in which event architecture, the theoretical project, did become built <u>form</u>, and for some, it has been claimed as part of a very specific type of architecture, the proto-icons of the icon type. To my mind, it is also the opposite; the unphotographable; the diffuse, the subjective, which is why straight formalists do not like it as much as they might. The forms' only purpose is to alert you to other systems of organisation that you can be interested in if you choose, or simply ignore.

Villanueva Brandt is right to say that the project is seminal. It set out clearly a kit of tactics as a way of generating a project. It still works as a model for experimental projects. It accurately predicted both formal and anti-formal strands of thought. It has many unpredictable children and grandchildren, who quarrel violently with each other. An iconic park, it is itself a contradiction in terms, and as such, partly a critique of the iconic generation that was to come. And it plays at something utterly new while reshaping something with a long history for a different time. And you can read that however you like.

FURTHER READING

Recommended reading for original competition details (text in French)

Alain Orlandi, Un Architecte/Une Oeuvre: Le Parc de la Villette de Bernard Tschumi, Paris, Somogy Éditions d'Art, 2001.

Alain Orlandi, La Villette 1971–1995: Histoires de Projets, Paris, Somogy Éditions d'Art, 1999.

Books

Jos Bosman, Bernard Tschumi: Architecture in/ of Motion, Rotterdam, NAi Uitgevers, 1997

Gilles Bure, Bernard Tschumi, Basel, Birkhäuser, 2008

Discourse of Events (Catalogue of exhibition held at the Architectural Association, London, 1983. Derived from work by students of Bernard Tschumi, Unit Master 1973–9 and Nigel Coates, Unit Master 1979–89.)

Gevork Hartoonian ed., Crisis of the Object: The Architecture of Theatricality, London, Routledge, 2006 (Includes Bernard Tschumi's essay 'Return of the Object'.)

Byeong Joon Kang ed., Film and Architecture: Busan Cinema Complex International Invited Competition, Seoul, Busan International Architectural Culture Festival Organizing Committee, 2006

Alexandra and Andreas Papadakis eds, Innovation: From Experimentation to Realization, London, New Architecture Group, 2003 (Features work by 20 contemporary international practices including Bernard Tschumi Architects.)

Andreas Papadakis, Theory and Experimentation: An Intellectual Extravaganza, London, Academy Editions, 1993

Cedric Price, Vaisseau de Pierres 2,: Parc de la Villette, Seyssel, Champ Vallon, 1987

Peter Rice, An Engineer Imagines, London, ellipsis, 1994

Bernard Tschumi, Architecture and Disjunction, London, MIT Press, 1994

Bernard Tschumi, Cinegramme Folie: Le Parc de la Villette, Paris' Nineteenth Arrondissement, Princeton NJ, Princeton Architectural Press, 1987

Bernard Tschumi, Event-Cities: Praxis, London, MIT Press, 1994

Bernard Tschumi, Event-Cities 2, Cambridge, MA, MIT Press, 2000

Bernard Tschumi, Event-Cities 3: Concept vs. Context vs. Content, Cambridge, MA, MIT Press, 2004

Bernard Tschumi, The Manhattan Transcripts: Theoretical Concepts, London, Academy Editions, 1994

Bernard Tschumi, Manifestos (Catalogue to accompany exhibition held at Architectural Association, London, 1979. Revised and expanded version of a catalogue entitled Architectural Manifestos, first published New York, Artists' Space, April 1978.)

Bernard Tschumi, Questions of Space: Lectures on Architecture, London, AA Publications, 1990

Bernard Tschumi, Tschumi on Architecture: Conversations with Enrique Walker, New York, Monicelli Press, 2006

Bernard Tschumi, Jacques Derrida, Anthony Vidler and Alvin Boyarsky, La Case Vide: La Villette (Publication to accompany the exhibition held at the Architectural Association, London, 1985.)

Bernard Tschumi and Roselee Goldberg, Space: A Thousand Words (Publication to accompany exhibition at the Royal College of Art, February–March 1975.)

Mark Wigley, Deconstructivist Architecture, Museum of Modern Art, New York, 1988

Articles on Parc de la Villette

Daralice D. Boles, 'New Architecture in Paris', special issue, Progressive Architecture, vol. 68, no. 7, July 1987, pp 67–99

'Close to the Madding Crowd; Architects: Bernard Tschumi', Building Design, no. 739, May 1985, pp 36–9

Jean-Louis Cohen and Monique Eleb-Vidal, '20th Century Architecture + Urbanism: Paris', special issue, A+U, no.9 supplement, September 1990, pp 6–265

Charlotte Ellis, 'Tschumi's Paris Follies; Architects: Bernard Tschumi', Blueprint, no. 52, November 1988, pp 40–1

'Fantastic Voyage; Architects: Bernard Tschumi', Building Design, no. 779, March 1986, p 15 (Review of an exhibition at the Architectural Association.)

Ziva Freiman, 'A Non-unified Field Theory; Architects: Bernard Tschumi', Progressive Architecture, vol. 70, no. 11, November 1989, pp 65–73

J. C. Garcias, 'Les folies Tschumi à La Villette' ['Tschumi's Follies at La Villette']; Architects: Bernard Tschumi, Domus, no. 703, March 1989, pp 12–15

'Glass Class; Architects: Cedric Price', Building Design, no. 853, September 1987, pp 34–7

George Hazelrigg, 'Living with Deconstruction; Architects: Bernard Tschumi with a Team of Landscape Architects and Artists', Landscape Architecture, vol. 95, no. 6, June 2005, pp 166, 168

Mark Hinshaw, 'La Villette after Twenty Years; Architects: Bernard Tschumi with a Team of Landscape Architects and Artists', Landscape Architecture, vol. 92, no. 8, August 2002, p 124

'International Competition for the Parc de la Villette (2); First Prizewinner: Bernard Tschumi', Architecture d'Aujourd'hui, no. 227, June 1983 Jun, pp 90–9

'Landscape', special issue, Building Design, no. 894, July 1988, pp 16–27

'Private View: Deconstructing a Modern Myth', Architects' Journal, vol. 187, no. 47, November 1988, p 97

Bernard Tschumi, 'AD Profile: Deconstruction in Architecture', Architectural Design, vol. 58 no. 3/4, March/April 1988, pp 6–80

Bernard Tschumi and Anthony Vidler, 'Bernard Tschumi', A+U, vol. 216 no. 9, September 1988, pp 9–68

'Bernard Tschumi', special issue, GA Document Extra, no. 10, 1997, pp 8–158

'Tschumi on Villette; Architects: Bernard Tschumi', Landscape Architecture, vol. 76, no. 3, May/June 1986, pp 86–7

'Tschumi's Prize-Winning Proposals for La Villette; Architects: Bernard Tschumi', Architects' Journal, vol. 177, no. 14, April 1983, pp 37–8

'Twentieth-Century Park', Casabella, vol. 47, no. 492, June 1983, pp 12–23

Thomas Vonier, 'Non-Parallel Parking', Progressive Architecture, vol. 74, no. 10, October 1993, pp 66–71

Mark Wigley, Bernard Tschumi and Jacques Derrida, 'Form; Being; Absence: Architecture and Philosophy', special issue, Pratt Journal of Architecture, vol. 2, Spring 1988, pp 4–228

Peter Wilson, 'The Park and the Peak – Two International Competitions. 1. Parc de la Villette, Paris; Equal First Prize Winners: Office for Metropolitan Architecture, and Bernard Tschumi', AA Files, no. 4, July 1983, pp 76–87

Related books, articles and commentaries

Architectural Association, The AA and the Imperial College of Science and Technology, London, AA Archives, 1964

Peter Cook, Drawing: The Motive Force of Architecture, Chichester, John Wiley & Sons Ltd, 2008, pp 23, 25–7, 36–40

Peter Eisenman ed., Five Architects: Eisenman, Graves, Gwathmey, Hejduk, Meier, New York, Oxford University Press, 1975

Peter Eisenman, Ten Canonical Buildings: 1950–2000, New York, Rizzoli, 2008

Peter Eisenman, Written into the Void: Selected Writings, 1990–2004, New Haven CT, Yale University Press, 2007

Eric De Jong ed., 'Superimposition of Points, Lines and Surfaces: A Park for the 21st Century', Landscapes of the Imagination, Rotterdam, NAi Uitgevers, June 2008, pp 128–35

Kate Linker, Vito Acconci, New York, Rizzoli, 1994

Cedric Price, 'ECHOES – Environment Controlled Human Operational Enclosed Spaces', AD, October 1969

Dan Reese, The Programmes of Architecture, London, Royal Academy of Arts School of Architecture, 2008, pp 83–9

Colin Rowe and Fred Koetter, Collage City, Cambridge MA, MIT Press, 1984

Manfredo Tafuri, Theories and History of Architecture, London, Granada, 1980

Manfredo Tafuri, Architecture and Utopia: Design and Capitalist Development, Cambridge MA, MIT Press, 1976

Carlos Villanueva Brandt, 'The Psyche of the Unit Master' in Paul Davies and Torsten Schmiedeknecht eds, An Architect's Guide to Fame, London, Architecture Press, 2005

Nigel Whiteley, Reyner Banham: Historian of the Immediate Future, Cambridge MA, MIT Press, 2002

Very many thanks are due to all the many people who helped us prepare this book for publication. In particular, we would like to thank Bernard Tschumi for his support for and input into the making of this book. Many thanks to Kate Linker for her detailed edits and Grace Robinson-Leo of Bernard Tschumi Architects for her invaluable and essential work in helping us to carry it through. Also, to our participating critics at the event, especially Bruce McLean for generously providing new and previously unpublished material for this book. From the Architecture Foundation we would specially like to thank Rowan Moore, Elias Redstone and Jade Niklai for their work on the original event and their support in developing the series. For their sterling contribution to the mammoth work of picture research, many thanks to Lauren Wright, Eliana Sousa Santos and Clare Hamman, who also provided general editorial support. At Routledge, we would specially like to thank Caroline Mallinder for her original support for the series, Katherine Morton and Ben Woolhead for continuing the work. At the University of Westminster we are particularly indebted to Kate Heron for her original support of the series, and especially to Professor Murray Fraser who provided detailed, tireless, extensive and stalwart advice, enthusiasm and criticism throughout. John Morgan and Michael Evidon from John Morgan Studio designed the original series and subsequently generously helped us oversee both this and Supercrit #3 and happily continue to design the stunning covers. Alex Lazarou took over the layout and fielded difficult font discussions with great good humour; thanks too to Alex and Toni for their hospitality. The book was made viable by funding from the University of Westminster, School of Architecture and the Built Environment.

Samantha Hardingham and Kester Rattenbury

INDEX

ILLUSTRATION CREDITS

**The authors and publishers would like to
thank the following individuals and
institutions for giving permission to
reproduce illustrations. We have made every
effort to contact copyright holders, but if any
errors have been made we would be happy to
correct them at a later printing.**

Page	Figure	Description	Credit
10–11	–	Supercrit #4 panorama	Alex Schramm
17	–	Perspective view	Bernard Tschumi Architects
18	–	Variants on organisational diagrams	Bernard Tschumi Architects
18	–	Area plan	Bernard Tschumi Architects
19	–	Exploded axonometric	Bernard Tschumi Architects
20–1	–	Four illustrated series	Bernard Tschumi Architects
22	–	Aerial view	Bernard Tschumi Architects
22	–	Distribution of the folies	Bernard Tschumi Architects
23	–	Site plan	Bernard Tschumi Architects
23	–	The 'Urbanism' document	Bernard Tschumi Architects
23	–	Cinematic sequences	Bernard Tschumi Architects
23	–	Diagrammatic plan	Bernard Tschumi Architects
24	–	Demonstration of folies on grid	Bernard Tschumi Architects
24	–	Computer renderings of folies	Bernard Tschumi Architects
25	–	The exploded folie	Bernard Tschumi Architects
25	–	Models of folies	Bernard Tschumi Architects
26	–	Watching a film	Sophie Chivet
26	–	Cinematic Promenade	Bernard Tschumi Architects
26	–	Listening to music	Sophie Chivet
27	–	The Parc as part of Paris	Xavier Bouchart
28	–	Perspective view of Folie N5	Bernard Tschumi Architects
28	–	Folie P6	J.M. Monthiers
28	–	Folie meets bridge	Peter Mauss
29	–	Intersection between bridge and folie	Peter Mauss
30	–	Aerial view collage	Bernard Tschumi Architects
31	–	Photocollage	Bernard Tschumi Architects
32	–	Fireworks display	Bernard Tschumi Architects
36–7	–	Event photos	Alex Schramm
39	–	Kate Heron	Alex Schramm
39	–	Samantha Hardingham	Alex Schramm
39	–	Paul Finch	Alex Schramm
39	–	Nigel Coates	Sophie Laslett
39	–	Murray Fraser	Alex Schramm
39	–	Peter Cook	Alex Schramm
39	–	Carlos Villanueva Brandt	Sue Barr
39	–	Bruce McLean	Courtesy of Bruce McLean. Concept Project: a party political speech on behalf of the Conceptual Party, Anthony d'Offay Gallery, 2002.
42	1	Poster for Supercrit #4	EXP
42	2	Pompidou Centre	Piano + Rogers
44	4	The Peak	Zaha Hadid Architects
44	5	Alvin Boyarsky	© Fred Rotkopf
44	6	Hillingdon Civic Centre	Will McLean
44	7	Archigram office	Kathy de Witt/RIBA
46–7	8	Nice Style	Courtesy of Bruce McLean
48	9	Paris, May 1968	Bruno Barbey/Magnum
48	10	New York State Theater	Lili Segal
48	11	Anton Furst	Glenn Shadix from 1990 Clock Series, www.glennshadix.com
48	12	Lutz Becker	Lutz Becker
48	14	Sketch for The Final Pose Piece	Courtesy of Bruce McLean
50–1	13	Notations from The Manhattan Transcripts	Bernard Tschumi Architects
52	15	'Joyce's Garden'	Bernard Tschumi Architects
52	16	Site photographs	Bernard Tschumi Architects
54	18	Koolhaas' competition scheme	Office for Metropolitan Architecture (OMA)
54	19	Hadid's competition scheme	Zaha Hadid Architects
54	20	Plan Voisin	Stuart Cohen and Steven Hurtt
56	21	Tabula rasa v genius loci	Bernard Tschumi Architects
56	22	Variants on organisational diagrams	Bernard Tschumi Architects
56	23	Superimposition	Bernard Tschumi Architects
56	24	Arrangement	Bernard Tschumi Architects
56	25	Competition board	Bernard Tschumi Architects

Page	Figure	Description	Credit
56	26	Exploded axonometric	Bernard Tschumi Architects
58	27	View along canal	Bernard Tschumi Architects
58	28	Intersection of bridge and folie	Peter Mauss
58	31	Neil Porter	Peter Guenzel
58	33	Peter Rice	Courtesy of Heidi Rice
58	35	Perspective drawing	Bernard Tschumi Architects
60	36	La Villette	Bernard Tschumi Architects
60	37	New York Central Park	Leonardo Susana
60	38	Stourhead	Mike Lane
60	39	Vito Acconci	Acconci Studio
60	40	Michel Foucault	Martine Franck/Magnum
60	41	Jacques Derrida	Ulrich Brinkmann
60	42	Sergei Eisenstein	Eugene Robert Richee/© Hulton-Deutsch Collection/Corbis
60	43	Battleship Potemkin	Sergei Eisenstein
62	44	Door, 11 rue Larrey	Marcel Duchamp /© Succession Marcel Duchamp/ADAGP, Paris and DACS, London
62	45	Automatic Drawing	© Photo Scala, Florence / MoMA
62	46	Vladimir Tatlin	Vladimir Tatlin
62	47	House VI	Dick Frank
64	48	'Extreme rigidity'	Bernard Tschumi Architects
64	49	Instant City	Archigram/Archigram Archives
64	50	MAGNET project	Courtesy of the Cedric Price Estate
64	51	'Erector Set'	Collection of Maproom Systems
64	52	Anni Albers	© Picture Scala, Florence / MoMA
64	53	Computer drawings	Bernard Tschumi Architects
66	55	Downsview Park	Bernard Tschumi Architects
68	56	National Theatre and Opera House	Bernard Tschumi Architects
68	57	Interface Flon	Bernard Tschumi Architects
68	58	Le Fresnoy Arts Centre	Bernard Tschumi Architects
70	59	Busan Multi-Media Cinema Centre	Bernard Tschumi Architects
70	60	Poster for 'Cheerful Architecture'	Will McLean, University of Westminster
70	61	Nestlé Headquarters	Eric Ed Guignard
72	62	Jean Nouvel	Gaston Bergeret
72	63	Bernard and Jean Tschumi	Courtesy of Bernard Tschumi
74	64	Paul L. Cejas School of Architecture	Bernard Tschumi Architects
76	65	Cedric Price and Bernard Tschumi	Courtesy of Bernard Tschumi
76	66	Logplug	David Greene/Archigram Archives
76	67	François Barré	Bernard Tschumi Architects
76	68	Serge Goldberg	Bernard Tschumi Architects
78	69	Tightrope walker	Bernard Tschumi Architects
80	70	Sound Distance of a Good Man	Bernard Tschumi Architects
80	71	High and Low	© David Salle/VAGA, New York/DACS
80	72	Untitled Film Still #17	Courtesy of the Artist and Metro Pictures
82	73	Opening day	Bernard Tschumi Architects
82	74	Unprogrammed Parc	Bernard Tschumi Architects
84	75	Pompidou Centre	Katsuhisa Kida
86	76	Transfer Station	George Trakas
86	77	Snow-covered Parc	Alessandro Palmacci
88	79	François Mitterrand	© Thierry Orban/Corbis Sygma
88	81	Cathedral of Brasilia	Marcelo Jorge Vieira
90	82	West Diaoyutai Tower	Bernard Tschumi Architects
92	83	Questions from the audience	Alex Schramm
96	84	'The whole Parc is a folly'	Sophie Chivet
96	85	Bernard Tschumi and the Queen	Bernard Tschumi Architects
98	86	Competition for the Bibilothèque Nationale	Futuresystems
98	87	Thames Gateway	Will McLean
100	–	Building Design	Building Design